FINANCIAL SECTOR OF THE AMERICAN ECONOMY

edited by
STUART BRUCHEY
UNIVERSITY OF MAINE

ᴀND SERIES

EXCHANGE RATES AND PRICES

THE CASE OF UNITED STATES IMPORTS

WILLIAM R. SMITH, JR.

GARLAND PUBLISHING, INC.
NEW YORK & LONDON / 1996

HB
235
U6
5635
1996

Library of Congress Cataloging-in-Publication Data

Smith, William Robert, 1953–
Exchange rates and prices : the case of United States imports /
William R. Smith, Jr.
p.   cm. — (The financial sector of the American economy)
Includes bibliographical references and index.
ISBN 0-8153-2373-5 (alk. paper)
1. Prices—United States. 2. Imports—United States. 3. Foreign
exchange rates. 4. Prices—United States—Mathematical models.
I. Title. II. Series.
HB235.U6S635   1996
382'.5—dc20   95-52989

Printed on acid-free, 250-year-life paper
Manufactured in the United States of America

Dedication

The completion of this project was one of the most frustrating tasks that I have ever undertaken. There were numerous occasions on which I made the decision to abandon it. Since the work is now complete I would like to express my gratitude to those people whose understanding and assistance made this work possible. It is dedicated to each of them.

The people who have suffered the most from my frustrations are my wife, Nora, and my sons, Derek and Damon. For my sometimes intolerable behavior and impatience I both apologize and express my appreciation for their understanding and tolerance. I love each of them very much and consider them to be the most important people in my life.

My mother, Wray Smith, became a terrific research assistant as she plowed through pages of data. Maybe I will be in a position to pay her for services rendered some day. My father, William R. Smith, Sr., is the very reason I became an academic and should be praised or damned as appropriate. I love both of my parents and thank them for the good they instilled in me.

I would also like to thank my friend Bob Headen for his guidance and understanding as he helped this study to unfold. This project would never have been completed without Bob.

Shannon Neal of the U.S. Department of Commerce in Greensboro, North Carolina is also deserving of much thanks. He made the collection of the import price data possible by taking time to learn the vagaries of the federal computer system in which these data were stored. I wish that all government employees were more like Shannon.

Finally, I would like to thank God for giving me my health and the strength and support of my wife, Nora. He sent her to me at a critical time in my life and I love and praise Him for this.

Contents

List of Tables

List of Figures

List of Abbreviations

ISIC	International Standard Industrial Classification
nes	not elsewhere specified
nspf	not specifically provided for
PPP	Purchasing Power Parity
PTM	Pricing to Market
SIC	Standard Industrial Classification
SITC	Standard International Trade Classification
TSUSA	Tariff Schedule of the United States Annotated
U.S.	United States
USITC	United States International Trade Commission

Exchange Rates and Prices

I

Introduction

The pricing practices of foreign producers that import into the U.S. market receive great attention from many observers of international business. The advent of floating exchange rates in the early 1970's for many advanced economies made the pricing of internationally traded goods a more complex proposition than had been the case under the Bretton-Woods regime of relatively fixed exchange rates. Businesspeople around the globe were forced to add the element of adjustments to exchange rate fluctuations to the myriad of other factors to be considered when establishing the prices of their products that would be sold in international commerce.

NEO-CLASSICAL THEORY AND THE PRICE-EXCHANGE RATE LINK

One theory as to how prices of internationally traded goods are related to exchange rates is termed purchasing power parity (henceforth PPP). PPP is grounded in the neo-classical model of perfectly competitive markets and is important because of the pervasiveness of the impact of this strain of economic theory on the thinking of many people in the industrialized world. People influenced by this tradition include leaders from business, academia, government, and labor. The press is also influenced by this theory base that is so ingrained in western economic thought. The following quote from a magazine of the popular business press serves as evidence:

> Japanese car makers . . . have raised their prices only about
> 29% since 1985, while the yen has climbed 115% . . .
> [*Money*, March 1988, page 86]

The Various Versions of PPP[1]

PPP at its most basic is referred to as the "law of one price." The underlying tenet is that identical products will cost the same in a given currency (other than relatively minimal differences for transportation costs and any relevant duties) regardless of the country in which they are being sold.

The implication of this strict version of PPP is that changes in exchange rates will be matched by proportional changes in the prices of traded goods (some possible exceptions will be mentioned below). In the above quotation concerning Japanese autos, the law of one price would imply that as the yen appreciated 115 percent against the U.S. dollar, the dollar prices of Japanese autos sold in the U.S. would also appreciate 115 percent. The failure of a proportional adjustment of import prices to such an exchange rate fluctuation to occur has often led to charges of unfair trading practices against some firms and even entire countries.

The absolute version of PPP is similar to the law of one price, but it uses price levels rather than prices of particular goods. Each good in a country's economy is weighted according to its importance in the economy. The resulting weighted price levels of each country are then equalized by an appropriate exchange rate. This exchange rate would take into consideration the respective inflation rates of the two countries in this process of equilibrating prices across the countries. If the law of one price holds for each good in an economy, then absolute PPP holds if the weights of each good in the two economies are the same, that is if each good is of equal relative importance to the economy in each country.

The most frequently used version of PPP is the relative version. This is more a matter of convenience than substance. Since most countries publish price indexes rather than prices of each individual good sold, relative PPP, with its calculation of a "theoretical" exchange rate based on changes in price indexes, is much easier to calculate than absolute PPP or the law of one price.

Is PPP the Answer?

There is no argument that changes in exchange rates and in the prices of traded products do occur. Regardless of which version of PPP is considered, the question of how, or whether, these changes are related begs for a theoretical answer. PPP is one such answer and its ability to explain actual pricing behavior in international markets will be examined further below.

FROM THEORY TO PRACTICE

While academic inquiry into the relationship between exchange rates and prices is important for the development of international pricing theory, businessspeople are more concerned with the potential impact of this relationship on the practice of business. Businesspeople involved in international markets indicate that pricing of their products is one of their major concerns. In a survey of U.S. executives whose firms operated internationally, Ricks and Czinkota (1979) found problems involving pricing in foreign markets to be the executives' second greatest concern in terms of the problems they were confronted with in those markets.

The finding of Ricks and Czinkota is a clear indication of the concern that international marketers have with the pricing element of their marketing mix. This global business community is also aware of the potential for dramatic repercussions in their competitive environment when significant exchange rate changes occur.[2] Their concern is with whether this potential impact becomes reality by changing international competitive balances.

PUBLIC POLICY RAMIFICATIONS

National governments are universally concerned with international trade issues. The economic well-being of a nation is directly affected by changes in its international trade flows. If prices for internationally traded products are subject to shifts due to exchange rate fluctuations the public sector is inherently concerned with the strength of the price-exchange rate relationship.

If a firm's prices in foreign markets show little or no responsiveness to exchange rate fluctuations the public sector in those markets is certain to raise questions. As demonstrated by the earlier example from the Japanese auto industry, the implication is that some form of dumping is occurring when the price-exchange rate relationship is weak. Dumping, or selling in foreign markets at prices lower than domestic prices, causes alarm in those markets. However, the possibility that dumping is predatory in nature (selling in foreign markets at prices below the cost of production in order to drive producers in the foreign market out of business) causes even greater concern and often leads to strained relations between the countries involved.

PASS-THROUGH AND EMPIRICAL RESEARCH

The relationship between import prices and exchange rates has come to be known in academic research as "pass-through" and can be defined as that portion of an exchange rate change that is reflected in import (or export) price changes. When a proportional relationship holds between import price changes and exchange rate changes pass-through is said to be complete and the rate of pass-through is 100 percent. For example, a ten percent increase in exchange rates (expressed as units of the domestic currency per unit of foreign currency) is accompanied by a ten percent increase in import prices when pass-through is complete (these changes would be in opposite directions if the exchange rate were expressed as foreign currency per unit of domestic currency but would be equal in absolute percentage to the change when exchange rates are expressed as above). If prices do not respond at all to exchange rate fluctuations, then pass-through is zero. When the rate of pass-through falls between zero and one hundred percent pass-through is said to be partial or incomplete.

Empirical research into the pass-through phenomenon began in the late 1960's with a Ph.D. dissertation by an economics student at Stanford University (Dunn 1970). Dunn's seminal work examined a period in the 1950's and 1960's when Canada experimented with a system of floating (or flexible) exchange rates.

Several additional empirical studies of pass-through were inspired by the one-time adjustment of otherwise fixed exchange rates by the U.S. in 1971 (commonly referred to as the Smithsonian agreement). The abandonment of the Bretton-Woods scheme of fixed exchange rates in 1973 eventually served as a catalyst for additional empirical research of pass-through behavior in the 1980's.

While the number of empirical studies is limited and much of the research has problems that will be examined below, the common thread that runs through the research is that the response of prices of traded products to exchange rate changes is not always proportional. This departure from expectations has led to dissatisfaction with the law of one price specifically and the perfectly competitive markets model generally. New theoretical explanations of observed pass-through behavior were called for.

RECENT THEORETICAL DEVELOPMENTS

One economist began to question the assumption that pass-through would always be complete as early as 1949. In a seminal theoretical work that began a departure from the perfectly competitive markets model as the basis for discussion of international trade issues, Haberler (1949) suggested the possibility of incomplete pass-through. He concluded that demand and supply price elasticities that were not infinite could cause the response of prices of traded goods to changes in exchange rates to be less than proportionate.

Even though pass-through was not specifically mentioned in Haberler's early work, the implication to be drawn was that incomplete pass-through was certainly possible. However, the real impetus for theoretical development in this area was the above mentioned empirical studies and their findings that challenged the law of one price and the perfectly competitive model.

Most of the theoretical developments of recent years that deal with incomplete pass-through fall under the rubric of the imperfectly competitive markets model and are grounded in the industrial organization literature. While these theoretical arguments will be reviewed in detail below, the general argument of Krugman (1987) and others is that market structure and other market-related conditions and concerns often lead international competitors to engage in incomplete pass-through. Krugman (1987) refers to this pricing behavior that entails incomplete pass-through as "pricing to market (PTM)" and has presented one of the most complete theoretical arguments on this issue.

In addition to those theoretical explanations of incomplete pass-through that are grounded in a model of imperfect competition, explanations of such behavior under the assumptions of perfect competition have also been advanced. These arguments will also be explained below in the literature review.

THE BASIC PURPOSE OF THE STUDY

The fundamental purpose of this study is to determine the impact of exchange rate fluctuations on the pricing practices of foreign industries that import into the United States market. This purpose will be pursued in the empirical tradition of several previous pass-through studies. However, the approach of this study will be different from those of earlier empirical studies in several regards in an attempt to make the findings more useful to both practitioners and academics.

Differences in Research Approach and Design

The limited amount of empirical research that has examined pass-through has been done almost exclusively at very high levels of aggregation. This means that the products being studied were aggregated to an economy-wide basis, or to the one- or two-digit level of various product classification schemes (such as Standard Industrial Classification, or SIC). This sort of aggregation leads to severe or complete loss of product identity.

Some of the researchers that have attempted to examine somewhat more disaggregated data have made some interesting observations that relate to the aggregation issue. Fieleke (1985) found that, "price movements for certain commodities diverged sharply from the movement of the country's general, or average, price level." He continued by observing that, "No doubt the net result . . . is that the change in price competition facing U.S. producers has varied considerably from country to country and commodity to commodity." Hooper and Mann (1989) observed that, "This evidence for specific industries contrasts with the evidence from aggregate data . . . " as they were discussing their finding that pass-through for individual products was much lower than for economy-wide data.

Hatter (1987)[3] comments that, "Price behavior for many of the [disaggregated] commodity groups, however, was quite different from the overall average." She continued by saying, "The overall pattern . . . masked significant differences in price ... among the individual commodities." She had comments in at least two other places in this study that indicated a serious problem with highly aggregated data masking some important differences between the products at finer levels of aggregation.

Mann (1989) stated, " . . . that more work with disaggregate data would be valuable. First, the aggregate data on export price behavior is often at odds with what apparently is the industry level behavior. Second, the analysis revealed that aggregate exchange rate data do not exhibit the great increase in exchange rate risk faced by the exporter at the industry level. Aggregate exchange rate data do not incorporate most of the developing world yet this area accounts for 20 to 40 percent or more of export value. Further work should investigate how best to integrate the developing countries, especially the high inflation countries, into the analysis."

These kinds of warnings cannot continue to be ignored in research involving international trade issues. The consequences of this neglect for consumers of such research are potentially disastrous. Basing management decisions on research that does not account for these issues could lead to grievous consequences for the firms involved.

The present study will describe the relationship between exchange rate changes and price changes made by U.S. importers at a very fine level of aggregation; specifically, at the seven-digit level in the Tariff Schedule of the United States Annotated classification scheme (TSUSA). There is no finer level of aggregation available for U.S. imports. As evidenced above, Mann (1989) has certainly been a strong advocate of such a disaggregated approach.

A second difference between this and most earlier pass-through studies will be the use of bi-lateral exchange rates. The use of highly aggregated data on import (or export) prices in previous studies led most researchers to utilize some type of composite, or basket, of the exchange rates of the world's major trading countries in their models. This resulted in a multi-lateral exchange rate being created. Since all exchange rates are bi-lateral (or country specific) by definition and the data on U.S. import prices utilized in this study will be broken down by country, the decision was made to utilize bi-lateral exchange rates. This will allow the analysis to focus on specific competitors and their individual pricing responses to exchange rate fluctuations.

Mann's (1989) observation that developing nations were systematically excluded from empirical studies of pass-through behavior led to another departure from convention in the present study. Several developing countries are major trading partners of the U.S. and account for a large percentage of total U.S. imports. Several of these countries will be included in the present study (e.g. Mexico, Brazil, South Korea, and Malaysia). This should make for a more representative sample of trading partners and point to any problems inherent in including such countries in a study of pass-through behavior.

The final major departure from earlier empirical studies of pass-through concerns the size of the sample of products to be examined. Earlier studies that attempted some degree of disaggregation studied a very limited number of products (typically two to eight). The present study will examine over 100 different products at the very fine level of aggregation mentioned above.

In summary, the principal differences in research approach/design of the present study from most earlier empirical studies of pass-through behavior are: (1) a much finer level of aggregation in the sample of U.S. imports, (2) the use of bi-lateral, rather than multi-lateral, exchange rates, (3) the inclusion of several developing countries in the sample, and (4) a much larger sample of imports. This is a combination of research attributes that, to the author's knowledge, has not been utilized in any previous empirical pass-through study. The inclusion of these attributes should yield results that are more useful to international marketers and indicative of some of the problems inherent in micro-level pass-through research.

Contributions of the Research

A detailed examination of the response of prices to exchange rate fluctuations is needed for several reasons. Such a study will assist in the advancement of pricing theory in an international context. The present study will afford an opportunity to test whether some of the recently advanced theories regarding pass-through behavior seem to explain this behavior better than the law of one price and the perfectly competitive model. Specifically, the PTM hypothesis of Krugman (1987) will be discussed in light of the findings of this study.

Perhaps more pragmatically, the present study should assist businesspeople in predicting the pricing responses of their international competitors to exchange rate changes. Anecdotes, such as the one above from *Money* magazine, have been the principal source of information available to marketers in the past and they may not be reflective of the actions of large numbers of international marketers in response to exchange rate changes.

The magnitude of exchange rate fluctuations in recent years also points to the importance of this research project. Table 1.1 and Figure 1.1 demonstrate that the degree of exchange rate fluctuations over the period to be examined in this study has been substantial. Table 1.1 indicates that even monthly changes can be dramatic. However, the changes over extended periods of time can be even more spectacular. Figure 1.1 demonstrates that from early 1985 to early 1988 the value of both the yen and the mark *vis-a-vis* the U.S. dollar increased by over 100 percent. If international marketers do make price changes in response to these fluctuations these changes could be substantial and have a great impact on the firm's international price competitiveness. If firms do not respond to these sometimes extreme fluctuations the potential for an impact on profitability is great.

While studies utilizing highly aggregated data may be useful from a macroeconomic policy perspective, they are of little relevance to firm or industry level decision makers. Marketers need to know how competitors in their specific product markets respond to exchange rate fluctuations, not how the overall economy or some broad-based industrial sector will respond in the aggregate to such developments. An examination of the relationship between exchange rates and import prices at its simplest level, that is examining import prices at the finest level of aggregation possible on a country-specific basis should make this study both unique and useful.

In this attempt to push back the boundaries of ignorance the warning of Monroe and Mazumdar (1988) will also be considered. They observed that, "It is necessary to utilize economic concepts and analytical methods, but at the same time to avoid falling into the trap of being enamored with the mathematical elegance of the structure and ignoring whether real progress in knowledge development has actually occurred." As will be discussed further below, this concern will lead to the use of a somewhat simplistic model for the measurement of pass-through in this exploratory stage of research.

In this same collection of pricing works that Monroe and Mazumdar contributed to, the editor, Devinney (1988), commented that, "Pricing strategy research has three primary components: the building of theoretical models to explain observed behavior, the empirical testing of those theoretical models, and the development of normative rules based on the tests of the theoretical models." In outlining this process, Devinney left out the critical initial component: the behavior must be *observed* in a methodical fashion.

Devinney himself later remarks in this same collection of works that, "A great deal of recent economic- and marketing-based pricing research has ignored the positive tradition on which it was based. One is reminded that Adam Smith based much of his economic theory on the pure observation of what was actually happening in markets, not what he thought should have been happening under ideal circumstances." This sort of observation is what much exploratory research is all about.

Since the critical first step of extensive methodical observation at the finest levels of aggregation has not been taken in the study of the response of international prices to exchange rate changes, it seems that such a step is necessary. This study of the response of U.S. import prices should serve to accomplish at least some part of that initial step.

RESEARCH QUESTIONS

The key issue to be examined is the following:

Do foreign (non-U.S.) firms adjust the prices of their imports into the U.S. in response to fluctuations in foreign exchange rates and, if so, how?

This issue will be examined through the use of a more detailed formulation of the basic model below:

Import Price = f(Foreign Price, Exchange Rates)

The model simply states that import prices are a function of the price of the product in its home country's currency and the rate of exchange between that currency and the currency of the importing country. While there are variables other than foreign prices and exchange rates that likely affect import prices (such as production costs), it is necessary to first explore this most basic relationship.

A more complete model can be developed once the basic issue has been examined. This research is exploratory by definition since it studies imports at a finer level of aggregation than any previous work of this scope. A parsimonious model seems in order at this stage. This model will be explained in greater detail below.

Encompassed within the broader scope of the above stated research question are additional questions that will be addressed to some extent by the present research. These questions will also be explained in detail below but will concern the following issues: (1) does there seem to be a lag structure to the response of prices to exchange rate fluctuations, that is are the price changes made over a period of time rather than immediately, (2) do there appear to be differences across industries in responding to exchange rate fluctuations, (3) do there seem to be country-specific patterns in the pricing responses to exchange rate changes, and (4) do there appear to be differences in pass-through behavior for different product classes such as consumer and industrial products?

Table 1.1

Largest Monthly % Increases and Decreases in the U.S. Dollar Value
of the Currencies of Selected Countries for the Period 1978-1988

Country	Largest % Increase	Largest % Decrease
Belgium	6.85	8.00
Brazil	0	29.76
Canada	2.37	3.40
France	6.93	9.34
Germany, W.	6.89	6.77
Hong Kong	9.11	10.29
Italy	6.15	7.00
Japan	9.38	6.30
Korea, S.	2.58	19.83
Malaysia	4.28	2.99
Mexico	10.29	60.81
Netherlands	6.85	7.11
Philippines	3.95	24.54
Singapore	4.04	2.62
Spain	6.14	6.36
Sweden	5.21	14.99
Switzerland	7.99	8.63
Taiwan	10.67	8.32
Thailand	2.25	15.56
United Kingdom	9.83	5.78

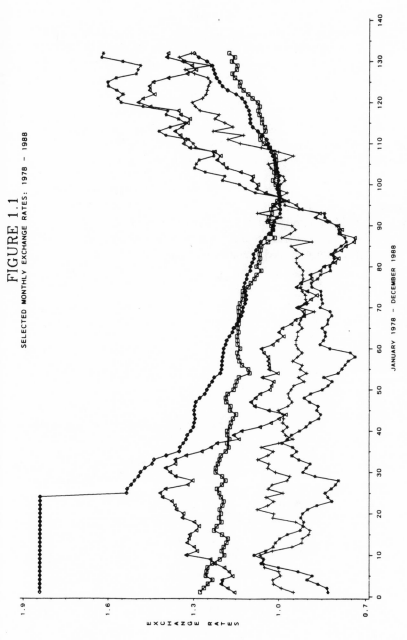

FIGURE 1.1

SELECTED MONTHLY EXCHANGE RATES: 1978 - 1988

JANUARY 1978 - DECEMBER 1988

YEN=● MARK=TRIANGLE CANADIAN DOLLAR=SQUARE KOREAN WON=DIAMOND TAIWANESE NEWDOLLAR=+

NOTES

1. Much of the discussion of PPP and its various forms in Chapters One and Two is based on Chapter 8 of *International Financial Markets*, Elsevier, New York, (1986) by J. Orlin Grabbe.

2. For a detailed exposition of some of the major reasons that exchange rates might affect international competitiveness see *Floating Exchange Rates and U.S. Competitiveness*, Publication #1332, U.S. International Trade Commission, December 1982.

3. This study does not deal specifically with pass-through. Hatter examines profit margins on U.S. exports for the period 1981-1986. As will be explicated further below, changes in profit margins of firms involved in international trade are an indication that they are not fully passing through exchange rate changes.

II

Literature Review

When one contemplates the response of import prices to fluctuations in foreign exchange rates there is an implicit assumption that exchange rates will fluctuate. This assumption would not always be appropriate since there are conditions under which exchange rates fluctuate little, if any. Since the type of exchange rate regime that is prevalent in countries involved in international trade could conceivably affect pass-through behavior, the various types of exchange rate regimes that might be adopted by a country will be discussed prior to the review of conceptual and empirical research dealing specifically with pass-through.

CURRENCY REGIMES

The control of a country's money supply is one of the most effective methods that a national government has for maintaining domestic political control and international sovereignty. One of the choices that a central government must make in terms of its money supply is whether to allow its currency to fluctuate in value against the currencies of other nations.[1]

A foreign economic policy under which currency fluctuations are allowed to occur in response to private market forces is known as a freely floating or flexible exchange rate regime. There are modifications of a freely floating regime that are designed to prevent violent fluctuations and allow for a more controlled rate of change in exchange rates. Such systems are referred to as managed floating regimes and involve interventions in currency markets on a regular basis by the central banking authority of the country adopting such a system.

At the opposite extreme of the spectrum of exchange rate regimes from the freely floating system is a system of fixed exchange rates. In such a regime the value of a nation's currency is set at a fixed rate against the currencies of all other nations. Fluctuations against other currencies outside of a defined acceptable band are prevented by central bank intervention. Pass-through would not be an issue in this system as long as the country's central bank is successful in its interventions.

There are, however, occasions on which adjustments in exchange rates are necessitated under a fixed system. A downward adjustment in a currency's exchange rate is termed a devaluation while an upward adjustment is termed a revaluation. Pass-through would become a concern under a system of fixed exchange rates in the event that a devaluation or revaluation became necessary. Arguments as to the relative merits of fixed versus floating exchange rate regimes will not be presented here. However, most economists seem to agree that a fixed exchange rate regime is less desirable than a flexible regime under most circumstances.

Some countries follow the practice of "pegging" the value of their currency (home currency) to that of another nation (or group of nations). This simply means that a fixed exchange rate is established between the currencies of the two nations. Some people perceive that this means the nation pegging its currency has established a fixed exchange rate regime. This is normally not the case. If the currency of the nation to which the home currency is pegged is allowed by its government to float, then the home currency will be fixed only against this currency to which it is pegged. It will effectively float against all other currencies.

A variation of pegging is referred to as a "crawling" or "creeping" peg. Under such a system, the currency of a country is pegged to that of another country (or basket of currencies) for a certain period of time. As the values of the two currencies begin to become misaligned the value of the pegged currency is allowed to change to a new fixed rate against the target currency. These adjustments are often necessary on a frequent basis under such a regime.

As will be explained below, the time period to be examined in this research was one in which the currencies of many of the world's major industrialized countries were under freely floating or managed floating regimes. The complete abandonment of the Bretton-Woods arrangement in 1973 led to the predominance of floating rates. Choosing to examine a period of floating exchange rates was based primarily on the fact that this is the system under which international marketers will most likely operate for the foreseeable future in many of the world's most important markets.

THEORETICAL FOUNDATIONS: PURCHASING POWER PARITY

Prior to reviewing the conceptual and empirical literature dealing specifically with pass-through, some background material on the conceptual heritage on which much of the thinking concerning pass-through was based until recently will be provided. This additional discussion of PPP and its foundations in the perfectly competitive markets model could prove useful in the formulation of a framework from which the pass-through literature can be reviewed.

An important initial observation is that the micro level focus of the present study dictates that the law of one price version of PPP be utilized. The relative version is clearly not appropriate for examining industry-level pricing data at fine levels of aggregation since it calls for the use of a price index that is calculated at an economy-wide level. The use of the absolute version of PPP would serve to do nothing more than complicate the measurement of pass-through for specific products since its use would require the calculation of the relative weights of importance of the products being studied to the economies of the countries involved. The calculation of such weights is burdensome and accomplishes nothing in this sort of measurement process.

The implication of the law of one price is that at any one point in time, the selling price of a specific product in one country (expressed in that country's domestic currency) will equal the selling price in another country (also expressed in its domestic currency) multiplied by the exchange rate for the currencies of the two countries. Thus the following static relationship would exist between a product's price in an exporting country, its price in an importing country (in this study, the U.S.), and the exchange rate for the currencies of the exporting and importing countries if the law of one price were to hold:

$$P_{us} = P_{for} * E$$

where P_{us} = U.S. \$ price of the good in the U.S.

P_{for} = foreign currency price in the foreign market

E = exchange rate between the two currencies

This "law" implies the following assumptions: (1) no transactions costs when buying in one market and selling in another, (2) no barriers to trade, (3) goods traded internationally are homogeneous, and (4) all countries are small enough that their demand for a product will not influence the world price. In other words, the law of one price assumes that perfect competition exists in international markets.

While the predominance of the perfect competition assumption has been reduced over the past two decades in academia, its influence on society at-large is still considerable. The importance of PPP in developing societies' attitudes toward the interaction of exchange rates and prices is evidenced by the following quote from Dornbusch and Krugman (1976): "Under the skin of any international economist lies a deep-seated belief in some variant of the PPP theory of the exchange rate." If economists teach PPP and students do not fully grasp the nuances of the concept (such as hidden assumptions), there is potential for its misapplication.

It seems that most, if not all, of the above listed assumptions inherent in the law of one price would not hold in today's international economy. For example, there are certainly transaction costs involved in trading and trade barriers seem to be on the increase today. However, as will be detailed in the development of the pass-through measurement model used below, some of these assumptions may not be very troublesome in this study. The assumption that the countries involved are small in an economic sense may prove to be the most problematic in this study.

Failures to explain the behaviors of exchange rates and prices have been cited for all versions of PPP (research through the early 1980's is reviewed by Officer (1982), who found inconclusive results with some studies finding that some form of PPP held well in a certain time period and not very well in others). However, the criticisms of the law of one price version are especially noteworthy in the context of the present study. Such criticisms are grounded in the law's failure to hold true in empirical research.[2]

While PPP's strongest advocates do not claim that it is a complete theory of exchange rate determination (even in the long-run), it is one of the simplest, most popular, and most durable explanations of exchange-rate fluctuations. None of the more complex theories of exchange rate determination (e.g. the money based theories) has proved any more accurate in predicting exchange rates. If one conclusion could be reached from the cumulative research on PPP in its various forms, it would probably be that PPP does not do a very good job of predicting exchange rates or pricing behavior in the short-term. However, there may be a general tendency for exchange rates to move toward PPP levels in the long-term.

The impact of the law of one price on the thinking of businesspeople, business analysts, union leaders, and public policy makers becomes apparent when observing their reactions to import price changes that occur subsequent to exchange rate changes. Many of these people feel that if a foreign currency appreciates in value 100 percent against the U.S. dollar, the dollar price of that country's products should increase by 100 percent, or at least very close to it. They are quick to level charges of unfair trading practices if such a response does not occur. This is an example of the misunderstanding of PPP that was alluded to above. Even under the assumptions of perfect competition and the law of one price, there exists the possibility that pass-through would be incomplete. This is discussed further below. However, the lack of viable alternative explanations for exchange rate behavior and a general belief that product arbitrage will equilibrate prices internationally may explain why the law of one price continues to exert an influence on the thinking of so many when the impact of exchange rates on prices is discussed.

A CONCEPTUAL VIEW OF INCOMPLETE PASS-THROUGH

Prior to discussing empirical pass-through studies it seems appropriate to examine the present state of theory regarding this phenomenon. As mentioned above, Dunn (1970) found in his seminal empirical work that pass-through was not necessarily complete. This and later findings of incomplete pass-through (e.g. Schwartz and Perez (1974)) demanded an explanation. Competing explanations for incomplete pass-through have developed over the past two decades and they will be examined further below.

Imperfectly Competitive Markets Explanation

Dunn (1970) made the following observation on pass-through: "It seems clear that no model which assumes perfect competition can explain how industrial prices would react to a flexible exchange rate."

With this observation Dunn laid the foundation on which much future pass-through research, both conceptual and empirical, would be based.

Dunn noted that in those markets examined in his research there was not, "a close relationship between changes in the exchange rate and changes in . . . prices." He continued by saying that, "Firms . . . apparently allowed export profits to absorb the effects of exchange rate variations. Since such behavior would be impossible in competitive markets, the results suggest that international trade theory would be more realistic and useful if provisions were made more often for the effects of imperfect market patterns."

The basic assumption of this latter group was that markets are imperfectly competitive. While there are several variants of this imperfect competition explanation, they are all rooted in the tenets of the industrial organization literature.

Branson (1972) provided the first thorough theoretical treatment of incomplete pass-through based on the assumption of imperfectly competitive markets (Haberler (1949) touched on the pass-through concept in an imperfectly competitive setting in a peripheral fashion in his theoretical work on foreign exchange markets but made no attempt to refine these ideas since the focus of his work was foreign exchange markets). He demonstrated that the extent to which pass-through would be incomplete depends on the supply and demand price elasticities for imports (Branson actually examined the behavior of export prices in response to exchange rate fluctuations, but the argument for import prices is analogous). Branson demonstrated that if import supply elasticities are infinite (perfectly elastic), as they are at the firm level under the assumptions of perfectly competitive markets, the rate of pass-through would always be 100 percent (by analogy, if import demand elasticity is infinite the pass-through rate would be zero if supply elasticity is anything less than infinite). Import supply elasticities less than infinity will result in incomplete pass-through. The degree of pass-through for products whose import supply elasticity is less than infinite will depend on both the degree of import supply elasticity and import demand elasticity (see Table 2.1 for the pass-through rates that Branson posited would result theoretically from various combinations of demand- and supply-price elasticities). The theoretical implications of these findings are that: (1) the higher the import supply elasticity in absolute terms (with demand elasticity constant), the higher the pass-through rate will be, and vice-versa, and (2) the higher the import

Table 2.1

Ratio of U.S. Import Price Change to Percentage Revaluation
in Dollar Terms, by Elasticities of Demand and Supply

Elasticities of Supply	Elasticities of Demand				
	-1.0	-2.0	-3.0	-5.0	-10.0
1.0	0.50	0.33	0.25	0.17	0.09
2.0	0.67	0.50	0.40	0.29	0.17
5.0	0.83	0.71	0.63	0.50	0.33
10.0	0.91	0.83	0.77	0.67	0.50
Infinite	1.00	1.00	1.00	1.00	1.00

Source: Branson (1972).

demand elasticity in absolute terms (with supply elasticity constant), the lower the pass-through rate will be, and vice-versa. Since perfect competition implies that both supply and demand price elasticities are infinitely elastic, the empirical results that found pass-through rates of less than 100 percent (e.g. Dunn (1970)) led several theorists to believe that the perfectly competitive markets model failed to offer an adequate portrayal of reality.

As mentioned above, the explanation for incomplete pass-through that evolved from this school of thought was grounded in the industrial organization literature. The distinguishing feature of the industrial organization paradigm is the structure-conduct-performance hypothesis. The proposition is that an industry's market structure (e.g. monopolistic) dictates its conduct (including pricing), which in turn determines its performance (profitability).

According to Scherer (1980), there are at least six major aspects of an industry's market structure. He suggests that these aspects are: (1) the extent of market domination by sellers, (2) the degree of vertical integration, (3) the extent to which firms are diversified across product lines, (4) the height of entry barriers (some authors also include height of exit barriers), (5) the extent of product differentiation, and (6) the degree of buyer concentration. Several of these aspects of market structure have been considered as potential explanators of pricing behavior in both domestic and international contexts. There has been a tendency to concentrate on two of these aspects of market structure in previous pass-through research: (1) the extent of market domination by sellers (normally utilizing concentration ratios as a proxy for this concept), and (2) the extent of product differentiation. This may be explained by the fact that market domination is the only one of the six aspects of market structure that has a somewhat adequate and readily available proxy (concentration ratios). The other aspects, including the extent of product differentiation, are simply too difficult to proxy.

If Scherer's six major aspects of market structure are examined closely, one will realize that they are all related to two basic concepts: (1) the price elasticity of supply, and (2) the price elasticity of demand. For example, if sellers tend to dominate a market (as reflected by high concentration ratios), in all likelihood the price elasticity of supply will be high. High entry barriers might also tend to make sellers' supply elasticity high as they have little to fear from prospective entrants into their market. If a few large buyers purchase a large portion of an industry's output, the price elasticity of demand will likely be high. As Branson (1972) demonstrated, these two types of elasticity will theoretically determine the extent of pass-through for a particular product.

In the imperfectly competitive markets model, the underlying idea is that sellers can elect to increase or decrease their profit margins in response to exchange rate changes rather than passing through these changes in the form of increased or decreased foreign currency prices in foreign markets. Examples of papers that have espoused this explanation and base their theoretical explanations on a model of this type are Baldwin (1988); Dornbusch (1987); Fisher (1989); and Krugman (1987). As noted by Knetter (1989), these papers (he does not mention Fisher) do not share common assumptions about market structure. Knetter points out that the response of import prices to exchange rate changes ultimately depends on the convexity of the demand schedule that individual sellers perceive that they are confronted with.

The practices of product differentiation and price discrimination across different world-wide markets do not violate the underlying assumptions in the imperfectly competitive model as they did in the perfectly competitive model. For example, a firm in the United Kingdom faced with a depreciation of the U.S. dollar against the pound could decide that it is going to decrease the U.S. price of its product in pounds to offset the dollar depreciation and effectively maintain price stability in the U.S. market in dollar terms. The decision would be to avoid passing through the exchange rate change and instead, to "soak up" the change in the form of a decreased profit margin in pounds. The firm would not have to offer this lower pound price domestically or in other foreign markets unless the degree of price discrimination was large enough to encourage international arbitrage of the firm's product. The implications for a dollar appreciation are easily drawn if profit margins rather than foreign prices are allowed to fluctuate with the exchange rate.

Krugman (1987a) develops several alternative explanations of incomplete pass-through behavior. He terms his first possible explanation the "sunk cost model" and discusses it at three different levels. The basic idea is that a firm that wants to export will have to make substantial investments in order to do so. These investments could include such things as adapting the product to the foreign market and developing a marketing and distribution network. Since recovering the costs involved in such investments could be extremely difficult the firm would likely consider these costs to be sunk. This irreversibility of investment could make trade (including price) rather unresponsive to exchange rate changes and lead to incomplete (or zero) pass-through.

Krugman then moves to the second level of this "sunk-cost" explanation in which he emphasizes that firms do not have static expectations regarding exchange rates. Firms tend to feel that a fluctuation in one direction will ultimately be offset by a movement in the opposite direction. They would not perceive it to be in their best interests to jump in and out of foreign markets in response to every exchange rate movement.

Krugman's final level of explanation in the "sunk-cost" approach involves the claim that even if firms do not expect a regression to some "normal" exchange rate (as in the second level of this explanation), they will adopt a "wait and see" attitude. If exchange rates are volatile firms will be hesitant to enter new markets and to exit from existing markets. The uncertainty of future exchange rates in a volatile environment effectively desensitizes firms to them.

Firms simply do not want to give up hard-won market share positions due to exchange rate changes that are beyond their control. A foreign competitor may choose to engage in strategic pricing behavior when the U.S. dollar depreciates by refraining from raising prices in the

U.S. market so that its U.S. market share will not decrease. While Krugman (1987), Knetter (1989) and others focus on firms with large market shares when considering the above explanation for incomplete pass-through, it seems possible that a foreign firm with a small share of the U.S. market might also engage in this type of behavior. Such a firm might limit its pass-through of a dollar depreciation in order to remain price competitive as it attempts to increase its U.S. market share. However, Krugman warns that, "If the sunk-cost model is at all right, we need fancier modeling and fancier econometrics on trade than anyone has yet done."

Krugman (1987a) dismisses the possibility that the perfectly competitive model has any application in explaining observed behavior. He discusses the price discrimination that occurred during the dollar's huge appreciation from 1981 through 1985. The increase in U.S. dollar prices of European luxury automobiles imported into the U.S. market in the face of huge declines in European currencies against the dollar coupled with the fact the prices for these cars in Europe were basically stable created large differences between the prices of the same automobiles in the U.S. and Europe. This caused many individuals in the U.S. to bypass traditional channels of distribution by traveling to Europe to purchase a luxury automobile and arranging for transportation of the car back to the U.S. in order to save thousands of dollars.

The failure of European auto manufacturers to pass-through this major currency fluctuation in the form of lowered U.S. dollar prices was followed by the same type of reaction when the dollar began its spectacular descent in 1985. The dollar prices of many European cars were kept fairly stable at a time when even modest levels of pass-through would have resulted in drastic dollar price increases.

Krugman labels this sort of resistance to passing through of exchange rate fluctuations as "pricing to market." He argues that pricing to market involves both imperfect competition and dynamics which would confirm the importance of those international trade models that have abandoned the perfectly competitive markets assumption. In this context Krugman uses the term dynamics to indicate that when firms believe that a currency fluctuation is temporary they will not adjust their pricing behavior in response to the fluctuation until they are convinced of the long-term nature of such a change. This implies that if a static model were reality (which he clearly does not believe to be the case) and firms were "pricing to market," they would continue to do so even if a currency change were expected to last indefinitely.

Krugman then discusses six additional explanations for incomplete pass-through and the resultant phenomenon that he labeled pricing to market (hereafter PTM). He first discusses three static models after stating that it seems a priori unlikely that such an approach would be adequate as an explanation.

The first model discussed is the simple supply and demand approach grounded in the perfectly competitive markets model. Krugman summarily dismisses this model by claiming that it fails due to an inability to explain price discrimination across markets.

Krugman then moves to imperfectly competitive models. The conclusion for the model assuming monopolistic price discrimination is that this model can explain pricing to market if demand curves have the right shape. Krugman demonstrates mathematically that there will be no pricing to market in the constant elasticity case and that pass-through will always be less than 50 percent in the case of a linear demand curve (non-constant elasticity). He comments that, "It is disturbing to rely so heavily on the shape of demand curves, however."

In discussing the static model of oligopoly, Krugman is once again disturbed by the necessity for depending on what he terms "unrealistic assumptions." These critical assumptions are: (1) domestic and foreign firms produce perfect substitutes, and (2) competition is Cournot in form with each firm taking the other's deliveries to the market as given. Krugman states that a more realistic model would have firms producing differentiated products and engaging in Bertrand competition. He concludes by commenting that, "The general point is that there is no general point: . . . the perceived elasticity of demand . . . depends on the particular functional form . . ."

Moving to what he terms "dynamic" models (those in which the actual or expected duration of an exchange rate change will affect the extent of pricing to market), Krugman first discusses an explanation for incomplete pass-through that emphasizes supply-side dynamics. The basic idea is that pricing to market can result from temporary bottlenecks to changing import volume, for example increased marketing and distribution costs when dramatic demand increases occur in response to exchange rate induced price decreases. The effect on pass-through behavior in this case depends on how long the appreciation/depreciation has lasted and how persistent it is expected to be. Krugman ultimately dismisses this as an insufficient explanation in that it cannot adequately explain the emergence of gray markets.

The fifth model discussed appeals to the slow adjustment of demand to price changes. This is akin to the J-curve phenomenon that has been empirically verified in numerous studies. This phenomenon is caused by buyers refusing to change their buying patterns and sellers not changing their supply patterns immediately in response to price changes. Krugman's ultimate conclusion is once again that the viability of this explanation is contingent on functional form.

In the final model discussed, Krugman suggests the idea that the purchase of imported goods is a two-stage process. First, potential buyers decide whether to take the time and incur the expense necessary to enter the market for a product. If the decision is to enter the market the potential buyer must then decide whether to actually make a purchase and in what quantity. The result of such a process is that demand depends on the price that consumers expect to pay when the market entry decision is made as well as the actual price the consumer is ultimately confronted with.

Under these circumstances it is important for a firm to develop a reputation for having its products priced in a certain range and then to honor this price range when the consumer must actually make the purchase decision. Failure to stay within these "expected" price ranges would result in consumers not believing future price pronouncements and discourage them from taking the initial step of entering a market. Krugman feels that this final model has the greatest potential for explaining incomplete pass-through and the incumbent PTM but makes no claim that any of these models meets the need for the "fancier" modeling that he alluded to earlier.

Some of the explanations advanced for incomplete pass-through under the assumptions of imperfect competition are not nearly as comprehensive in nature as those discussed above. For example, Knetter (1989) mentions that one hypothesis would involve menu costs. He proposes that these costs involved in publishing revised price lists (menu costs) would tend to dampen the response to exchange rate fluctuations. A producer might hesitate to incur these costs if he perceived that an exchange rate fluctuation was transitory. The likelihood that menu costs are a major consideration in pricing behavior seems remote for many products but this could be a consideration in some situations.

Fisher (1989) has also done theoretical research on the pass-through question. His arguments are fairly comprehensive in nature and cover basically the same ground that Branson (1972) and Krugman (1987a) do. Fisher does, however, give a more extensive treatment to the possibility that the degree of product differentiation will affect pass-through. He demonstrates theoretically that with certain assumptions imposed the degree of product differentiation will affect pass-through behavior. However, his implication that many food products and semi-manufactures cannot be differentiated may be questionable. Frank Perdue's success in differentiating uncooked chickens serves as an example that even commodity-like products can be successfully differentiated.

Perfectly Competitive Markets Explanation

While Dunn's (1970) claim that allowing profits to absorb the effects of exchange rate changes was inconsistent with the notion of perfect competition is true, the implication that incomplete pass-through could not be explained in the context of perfectly competitive markets was questioned by several theorists (e.g. Dornbusch (1987)). The explanation that has been advanced focuses on the changes in import/export demand that might result from price changes that are initially caused by fluctuations in exchange rates.

An example of a situation under which changes in demand might create the appearance of incomplete pass-through would result when the currency of a large country (in an economic sense) such as the U.S. appreciates in value. If complete pass-through of a U.S. dollar appreciation occurs, the dollar price of U.S. imports would be reduced by the same proportion as the exchange rate change. However, this lower dollar price would result in an increase in U.S. demand for imported products. Since the large country (in this example, the U.S.) would account for such a large percentage of total world demand for the product, the world price of the product would increase. If the two parts of this process were to occur in rapid succession (virtually simultaneously), the decrease in price that results from the currency appreciation could be offset to some extent (or even completely) by the increase in price caused by the increase in demand.

The net result of this series of events in the large country case might be little or no apparent reaction of the price of the import to the currency fluctuation in the large country. The change in demand would, in effect, cancel out some or all of the effect of the exchange rate change. The results of a depreciation in the value of the currency of a large country are easily anticipated.

As sensible as this "large country" explanation of incomplete pass-through in perfectly competitive markets might appear, there is empirical evidence that non-competitive behavior does occur in international markets (see Herd (1987) for a review of some of these studies). Practices such as price discrimination across international markets by producers seem to be very common and, as Krugman (1987) asserts, such discrimination is simply not possible under the assumptions of perfect competition.

An Explanation Using No Market Structure Assumptions

While the above explanations are, to some extent, contingent on the type of market structure that is assumed (perfectly competitive, monopolistic, etc.), there is a third basic type of explanation for incomplete pass-through that requires no such assumption. This explanation is centered around the fact that an apparent lack of pass-through can actually be the result of changing foreign prices for a product that will be imported into the United States. The argument can be demonstrated mathematically as follows:

$$P_{us} = P_{for} * E$$

where P_{us} = U.S. \$ price of the imported good in the U.S.
P_{for} = foreign currency price in the foreign market
E = exchange rate between the two currencies

The above is again the static relationship that exists between foreign and domestic prices for a traded product and the exchange rate for the currencies of the importing and exporting countries at any one point in time for a specific product. For pass-through to occur, there must be a change in the exchange rate (E) since pass-through is a measure of the change in price of an imported product in relation to the change in the exchange rate. This leads to the taking of derivatives of each term with respect to time:

$\partial/\partial_t(P_{us}) = \partial/\partial_t(P_{for}*E)$, then let

$\partial/\partial_t(P_{us}) = \wp_{us}$ and

$\partial/\partial_t(P_{for}*E)=E*\partial/\partial_t(P_{for}) + P_{for}*\partial/\partial_t(E)=(E*\wp_{for})+(P_{for} * \ddot{E})$.

$\therefore \wp_{us} = (E* \wp_{for}) + (P_{for}*\ddot{E})$.

Dividing this derived equation by the original equation will yield percentage changes and leads to the following:

$\wp_{us}/P_{us} = (E* \wp_{for} + P_{for}*\ddot{E})/(P_{for}*E)$, which simplifies to

$\wp_{us}/P_{us} = (\wp_{for}/P_{for}) + (\ddot{E}/E)$.

Letting $\wp_{us}/P_{us} = \mathcal{P}_{us}$
$\qquad (\wp_{for}/P_{for}) = \mathcal{P}_{for}$ and
$\qquad (\ddot{E}/E) = \hat{E}$ leads to the following:

$\mathcal{P}_{us} = \mathcal{P}_{for} + \hat{E}$.

Dividing this equation through by $\hat{E}$ yields the following:

$\mathcal{P}_{us}/\hat{E} = (\mathcal{P}_{for} + \hat{E})/\hat{E}$.

The left hand term in the above equation is the measure of pass-through as it represents change in the price of U.S. imports in relation to the change in the exchange rate. This means that pass-through (PT) equals the following:

$PT = 1 + (\mathcal{P}_{for}/\hat{E})$.

This final relationship (measure of pass-through) means that as long as the term $\mathcal{P}_{for}/\hat{E}$ is equal to zero, then pass-through will equal one (100 percent), or be complete. However, when $\mathcal{P}_{for}$ is not equal to zero (i.e., when the foreign currency price of the imported product changes), the rate of pass-through will always be something other than 100 percent (if the change in the foreign price of the product is equal to the change in the exchange rate but in the opposite direction, as one would expect, the value of the term $\mathcal{P}_{for}/\hat{E}$ would be -1 and the result would be a pass-through rate of zero).

The principal conclusion to be drawn from the above algebraic manipulation is that pass-through could well be incomplete regardless of whether one assumes that competition is perfect or imperfect. Another important finding is that if exchange rates were perfectly reflective of differences in economy-wide rates of inflation between two countries, as would be predicted under the relative version of PPP, then pass-through would always be zero at the economy-wide level because the value of the term $\mathcal{P}_{for}/\hat{E}$ would always be -1 (i.e., changes in foreign prices would always be accompanied by an equal but opposite change in the exchange rate). This would mean that pass-through (PT) would be equal to $1 + (-1)$, or zero (refer to the final equation in the above manipulation). This would make the empirical examination of pass-through rather uninteresting if aggregate level data were used.

International Pricing Theory and Pass-Through

Even though some progress has been made in pricing models in the last fifty years, a comment made by J.R. Hicks in 1939 still seems appropriate today when examining the status of international pricing theory: "It is, I believe, only possible to save anything from this wreck . . . if we can assume . . . perfectly competitive markets . . . Personally, however, I doubt if most of the problems we shall have to exclude for this reason are capable of much useful analysis by the methods of economic theory."

Woo (1984) exemplifies the uncertainty surrounding the development of any generally accepted model of pass-through behavior: "Except for the simple doctrine of purchasing-power parity . . . theory predicts no overall correlation between exchange rate movements and price level movements." He continues by saying, "The key point is that there is no unambiguous relationship between the exchange rate and the price level." Even textbooks dealing with issues concerning international economics have recognized the reality of the situation as evidenced by the following comment:

> The predictions relating to price behavior that can be
> derived from . . . theories . . . are not always consistent
> . . .. This has focused attention on . . . empirical research.[3]

Krugman (1987a) lamented over the same problem as he concluded his theoretical development of alternative explanations for incomplete pass-through. He stated that, " . . . econometric models of trade that worked well during the first half of the 1980's have fallen apart in the second." Krugman continued by stating that, "What is needed at this point is not so much more theory as more data. Clearly the next step will have to be to focus on particular industries . . ."

EMPIRICAL RESEARCH

When reviewing the empirical studies of pass-through there are several ways in which they can be classified. The difference in classes of research necessitates the introduction of some background material prior to the selection of specific studies to be reviewed in the present work.

Effect of Exchange Regime on Pass-Through Studies

One way to classify empirical pass-through studies is by the type of exchange rate regime that predominated during the time period being studied. Most early studies examined the pass-through of one-time devaluations or revaluations of otherwise fixed exchange rates (Dunn (1970) was the exception as he examined a period in which the Canadian dollar was floating against the U.S. dollar). For example, there were several studies that examined the response of prices to the 1971 "Smithsonian" devaluation of the U.S. dollar prior to the complete collapse of the Bretton Woods arrangement for basically fixed exchange rates.[4] Such a one-time, relatively large, change in exchange rates could easily have a very different impact on the behavior of prices from that of the continual changes (often in very small increments) inherent in a system of floating exchange rates. For this reason only those studies which examined pass-through behavior during periods when the currencies of the major industrialized countries were floating in some fashion will be reviewed here.

Studies of Imports or Exports

Empirical studies of pass-through can also be classified as examining imports or exports. Studies of both imports and exports will be reviewed here even though the focus of this study is U.S. imports and there is quite possibly a difference in pass-through behavior for U.S. imports and exports. Such a difference in behavior could be due to the fact that U.S. imports are being sold into a market that is the classic case of a large country in economic terms, while most (if not all) U.S. exports do not go to such "large" countries. Foreign dependence on the large U.S. market as the principal outlet for many products could well affect the seller's pricing behavior in this market. For U.S. producers/exporters there is no foreign market on a par with the U.S. market in terms of importance.

Use of Disaggregated Data in Empirical Research

In previous empirical research there have been few attempts to examine pass-through at lower than the two-digit SIC (Standard Industrial Classification), SITC (Standard International Trade Classification), ISIC (International SIC), or TSUSA (Tariff Schedule of the United States Annotated) levels. The use of this type of highly aggregated data creates a problem with aggregation bias. This bias results principally from the heterogeneity of the products contained within such wide-ranging categories.

As Goldstein and Khan (1985) state, " . . . disaggregation is always better . . . " if such data are available. They even complain that in most studies when the author(s) recognizes a problem with aggregation bias there is no attempt to disaggregate beyond the one- or two-digit level of the data classification scheme being used. This is still a very high level of aggregation and calls into question the results of such studies.

Mann (1989) observes that, " Most recent empirical work is grounded in models of imperfect competition, yet tested using aggregate data. This mismatch would be less worrisome if the industry and aggregate data behave similarly." This use of aggregate data to examine micro-level models is troublesome and led to the decision to use TSUSA data at the 7-digit level in the present study. These data are compiled at the finest level of aggregation available in publicly distributed trade statistics. For example, at the seven-digit level, the SITC contains about 3,000 product categories, while TSUSA contains over 16,000.

Considering this micro focus, the review of the empirical literature will concentrate on those studies that utilized product data dissaggregated to at least the 4-digit level of one of the major product classification schemes (in reviewing studies utilizing highly aggregated data, Herd (1987) indicated that the results are inconclusive with pass-through rates across 11 studies ranging from 50 to 80 percent on an economy-wide basis). Studies initially utilizing data at the 4-digit (or higher) level that later resort to some sort of cross-product aggregation or pooling (e.g. Feinberg 1989) are not reviewed as these upward aggregation procedures effectively increase the level of aggregation to the 2- or 3-digit level. As will be discussed below, even products at the 4- or 5-digit level have been shown to have problems with aggregation bias.

Methods for Calculating Rates of Pass-Through

There are three methods that can be utilized for the calculation of pass-through rates. One method is based on the theoretical connection between import supply and demand elasticities and pass-through rates. Under this alternative, a researcher would empirically determine the supply and demand elasticities for imports and use these values in the manner described by Branson (1972) to calculate pass-through. However, the extreme difficulty encountered in determining import (or export) supply elasticities, as evidenced by the paucity of existing estimates of their values (see Goldstein and Khan 1984), makes the use of this method for arriving at empirical estimates of pass-through rates problematic.

The problems inherent in calculating pass-through rates indirectly through the use of import supply and demand elasticities led to the adoption of alternative methods. There are two methods for calculating pass-through directly from data on import prices and exchange rates.

The method that has been most prominently featured is a regression-based model. Using this method a researcher regresses import prices (or changes in import price changes) on the contemporaneous exchange rate (or change in the exchange rate). Some number of lagged values of the exchange rate variable are often included as regressors. The pass-through rate is then calculated as the sum of the regression coefficients of the contemporaneous and lagged values of the exchange rate variable. This pass-through rate is actually nothing more than the elasticity of prices with respect to exchange rates.

The reason for including lagged values of the exchange rate variable is that there are certain institutional lags (such as transport time and reporting lags) that could delay the impact of an exchange rate change on prices. Another reason is that there may be a reluctance on the part of sellers to pass-through all of a major fluctuation immediately. Spreading the pricing response over time might make the price changes (especially increases) somewhat more palatable to prospective buyers.

A major advantage of this approach is that the use of high-frequency data, such as monthly or weekly, could lead to results that provide useful information about the timing of the response of import prices to fluctuations in exchange rates. The use of these lagged values of the exchange rate variable allows this sort of dynamic adjustment process to be captured by the regression analysis. As will be noted below, a number of other explanatory variables (in addition to exchange rates) have been utilized in the regression models examining pass-through.

Another method used in calculating pass-through rates does not depend on regression-type techniques. This is sometimes referred to as the "end-point" method. Using this approach the researcher calculates the percentage changes in import prices and exchange rates that have occurred from the beginning to the end of the time period being examined. For example, if a researcher were interested in calculating this version of pass-through for the period of 1977 through 1982 he would begin by choosing some value for exchange rates and prices in 1977. This could be the first price (or exchange rate) quoted at the beginning of 1977, an average for the entire year or some sub-period thereof, or some other representative value. The researcher then does the same thing for the end-point in his time-frame (1982 in this example). Then the percentage changes that have occurred during the time period are calculated for both variables. The rate of pass-through using this method is then the quotient of the percentage change in import prices divided by the percentage change in exchange rates (expressed as a percentage).

With simplicity of calculation being its principal advantage, there are disadvantages to using these end-point pass-through rates. The principal disadvantage of this static approach is that it cannot account for the potentially large fluctuations in exchange rates and import prices that might have occurred in the time period between the two end-points. The results are then driven by the choice of the end-points or time period examined.

Studies Focusing on Macro-Level Issues

Finally, there is a distinction to be drawn amongst pass-through studies based on the objectives of the researcher(s) conducting the study. Several of the empirical studies that include some calculation of a pass-through rate do not focus on the pass-through issue. These macro-level studies include the calculation of a pass-through rate as a part of a broader examination of how exchange rate changes might affect the overall trade balance of a country. Studies whose principal focus is the examination of pass-through behavior are more useful to a firm-level decision maker since the pass-through rates calculated as a part of an examination of a macro-level trade model come from the use of economy-wide data. This literature review will examine only those studies in which the pass-through concept is the primary focus.

Studies Using Disaggregated Data and Flexible Rates

One study that would appear by the date of its publication to fall outside of an era of floating exchange rates was conducted by Dunn (1970). He examined the pass-through of fluctuations in the Canadian dollar/U.S. dollar exchange rate to the prices of Canadian exports to the U.S. and vice-versa. The time period studied coincided with Canada's experience with floating exchange rates between 1950 and 1962. This study was conducted at a time when the arguments concerning fixed versus flexible exchange rate regimes were fierce. Dunn's work had to draw more than a passing mention in this selective review of empirical research since it is the seminal empirical study of pass-through behavior.

Dunn's purpose in conducting this study was to "invalidate the argument that such a system [flexible exchange rates] cannot operate successfully for an open economy because too many prices will be forced to shift from day to day to offset exchange rate movements." The underlying theme of Dunn's work was that we do not live in a world where the ideal of perfect competition is a reasonable representation of economic reality. He argued that an imperfectly competitive world made the law of one price (and the frequent price adjustments that it would necessitate to accommodate exchange rate movements) inoperative in any real sense.

Dunn analyzed six products at a level that would approximate the 3- or 4-digit SIC scheme. Four of the products were raw or semi-processed materials (crude oil, gasoline, coal, and copper). The other two products were rolled mill products (steel) and window glass. Dunn concluded that his finding that none of these products exhibited high levels of correlation between changes in exchange rates and changes in prices supported his claim that a floating exchange rate regime would not lead to severe problems related to the necessity for frequent price adjustments on traded goods.

A study that has received little or no attention from subsequent researchers into pass-through behavior was conducted by the United States International Trade Commission (USITC) in September of 1983 under the direction of Reuben Schwartz. This lack of attention is evidenced by the fact that the study is not cited by any of the authors of pass-through works done subsequent to its publication in September of 1983, nor is it listed under exchange rates or pass-through in any of the standard data bases listing publications by subject heading (e.g. ABI Inform).

The USITC study is especially interesting in that it utilizes products disaggregated to the 7-digit TSUSA level (reaggregation by combining 7-digit TSUSA numbers prior to data analysis effectively transforms the 7-digit TSUSA data into 7-digit SITC data). The data are quarterly observations for 1977:1 through 1982:4 (24 observations).

As with most other studies utilizing a regression-based approach to calculating pass-through rates, the USITC group estimated their equations in log-log form (all variables transformed into natural logarithms). One strength of the study is that bi-lateral trade relationships (e.g. bi-lateral exchange rates) were examined as opposed to the use of data aggregated across several trading partners (e.g. a trade weighted basket of currencies). The regression model utilized included the use of a distributed lag of the exchange rate variable and a standard Cochrane-Orcutt procedure to address problems with serially correlated error terms.

In addition to the exchange rate variable and its lags, proxies for production costs, prices of U.S.-made substitutes, and non-price factors were included as explanatory variables in the pass-through measurement model in an effort to control for the effects of factors other than exchange rates on U.S. import prices. However, the authors indicated that the proxies utilized to represent some of these variables may have been somewhat questionable (e.g. producer price index as a proxy for costs and an index of foreign and domestic production as a proxy for the non-price factors). The results reported by the authors were those deemed to be the most satisfactory based on coefficient signs, significance levels, and coefficient behavior in the distributed lags.

Several of the findings of the USITC report are interesting. The study tends to confirm earlier work (e.g. Isard 1977) that found that the law of one price did not hold even for homogeneous products. The researchers also commented that pass-through seemed to occur more rapidly than had been indicated by earlier studies examining periods of fixed exchange rates with infrequent exchange rate adjustments. Finally, the measurements of pass-through rates for the U.S. imports studied were widely varied (see Table 2.2 for a summary of results).

The rate of pass-through for Japanese piano imports was .39 while that for German pianos was .59 and not statistically significant. Since the null hypothesis that the exchange rate coefficient was zero (which in this study implied complete pass-through) could not be rejected, this finding suggested that pass-through was 100 percent, or complete (the construction of the measurement model in this study caused the rate of pass-through to be the difference between one and the reported coefficient of the exchange rate variable, that is pass-through = 1 - reported coefficient). The rate of pass-through for brass strip imports from Japan was .27 while German imports of brass strip demonstrated negative pass-through. The final import examined was bicycles from Japan. The rate of pass-through for this product was also negative.

The counter-intuitive (negative) relationships were not commented on by the authors but could be explained several ways. This type of relationship might reflect the influence of non-exchange rate factors such as changes in production costs or changes in product characteristics. Froot and Klemperer (1989) raise the possibility that such a perverse relationship could conceivably be explained by the expectation that future exchange rate changes would be in the opposite direction of contemporary changes. The idea is that international traders are reacting to the anticipated direction of exchange rates rather than the present direction. The future value of profits received in a foreign currency could be dramatically impacted by exchange rate fluctuations so contemporary actions could reflect expectations of future exchange rates.

Kreinin, Martin and Sheehey (1987) took a different approach to the study of pass-through from that of any other researcher to date. They observe that, " . . . practically all empirical studies refer to a country's trade in the aggregate, without reference to differential performance across industries. By contrast, the theoretical literature explaining the commodity composition of international trade is increasingly concerned with industry and commodity characteristics, as the assumption of perfect competition is gradually replaced by that of monopolistic competition or oligopoly."

The objectives being pursued by Kreinin, et al were: (1) to examine the extent to which pass-through behavior varies across products and competitors/countries, and (2) to determine whether pass-through behavior is influenced by the characteristics/structure of the industries in which the products are traded. They claimed that these research foci dictated a departure from a regression-based analysis of import price and exchange rate time-series in favor of an analysis across a number of competitors/countries in various industries. The argument for the use of cross-sectional data to examine differences across industries seems self-evident. However, the argument against the use of time-series analysis seems somewhat suspect. Kreinin, et al apparently did not consider the use of a cross-section of time series. They might have advanced this argument as a justification of the type of approach they utilized in measuring pass-through.

As part of their unique approach, Kreinin, et al calculated pass-through rates as the percentage change in price over various periods of monotonic change in the U.S. dollar exchange rate. These calculations did not relate import price changes to changes in exchange rates. In fact, the magnitudes of the changes in exchange rates during the periods examined in the study were not considered in any way.

Even though Kreinin, et al chose to eschew the commonly used regression method for measuring pass-through, their failure to utilize some method that considers the magnitude of exchange rate fluctuations seems questionable. Many researchers would likely not consider the percentage change in price alone to be a pass-through rate. Kreinin, et al could certainly have calculated pass-through rates by the end-point method rather than with price changes only.

If Kreinin, et al had calculated pass-through rates using the price and exchange rate time series, the analysis across competitors/countries would have seemed appropriate. Their recognition of the necessity for a cross-sectional analysis in empirically testing their general hypotheses was a vital contribution of their work.

Kreinin, et al analyzed U.S. imports from the United Kingdom, Japan, and Germany (all references to Germany in this paper refer to data for what was West Germany). About seventy industries at the 4-digit SIC level were included in the sample (these industries were not identified). Once the authors had determined percentage changes in import prices (which they labeled as pass-through) for the various industries they relied on the industrial organization literature for guidance as to what concepts might explain differences in pricing behavior across industries. Proxies for the market structure of an industry, its profit margins, the degree of labor versus capital intensiveness, the human capital or skill levels in the industry, and costs were included as potential explanators of differences in pass-through behavior in this second stage of analysis.

The authors utilized the U.S. industry four-firm seller concentration ratio as an indication of market structure. They reasoned that the greater the U.S. market concentration of U.S. producers the more likely these U.S. producers are to react to price changes by their foreign rivals as they attempt to increase their U.S. market share. The idea is that in an oligopolistic situation the foreign producers will realize that any price reductions they make in response to exchange rate fluctuations will be matched by their U.S. rivals. This would serve as a disincentive for making these price changes. The authors thus reasoned that products traded in more concentrated markets would experience less than complete pass-through of exchange rate movements.

Kreinin, et al concluded that pass-through behavior varied across countries and was somewhat asymmetric for periods of exchange rate appreciation and depreciation. This asymmetric response to exchange rate changes indicated that foreign producers tended to pass-through depreciations of their currencies to a greater extent than appreciations (with their incumbent effect of increasing dollar prices in the U.S.). The authors pointed to actions and attitudes of U.S. distributors as the key factor causing this asymmetry to occur. They argued that the U.S. distributor would desire to have dollar appreciations passed through while resisting the pass-through of dollar depreciations.

The authors also interpreted their results to mean that some of the industry characteristics mentioned above (e.g. capital versus labor intensiveness) do influence the extent to which exchange-rate changes are passed through to import prices. However, they were surprised to find that the relationship between market structure (using the 4-firm concentration ratio as its proxy) and pass-through was statistically insignificant since they felt that this was the most important industry characteristic in the study. Researchers who feel that these concentration ratios are not an appropriate indicator of the market structure found in a particular industry might be less surprised (e.g. Krugman (1989), who amplifies the common criticism that these ratios based on the SIC scheme often over- or understate the actual degree of seller domination in an industry). The Kreinin, et al results could also have been somewhat driven by their choice of techniques for calculating pass-through.

Mann (1986) seemed to spark renewed interest in pass-through research. The activity in pass-through research had been minimal during the late 1970's and early 1980's and Mann's work seemed to arouse the curiosity of other researchers about the idea of pass-through behavior under a regime of floating exchange rates.

Mann (1986) analyzed some relatively disaggregated data (3- to 4-digit SIC level) but did not report pass-through results for these data. Hooper and Mann (1989) analyzed the same products examined in Mann (1986) and did report their pass-through measurements. Even though the 3- to 4-digit SIC level of aggregation certainly is better for micro-level studies than economy-wide or 1- or 2-digit levels, there is still a great danger of problems with aggregation bias.

The sample period of the Hooper and Mann (1989) study was 1977:1 through 1986:4 for a total of 40 quarterly observations. While this study does attempt some disaggregation, the authors do not allow for possible differential pricing behavior on the part of various international (i.e. country) competitors. The overall imports of the seven products are examined with no attempt being made to look at the data on a country-by-country basis. This dictates that the exchange rate variable utilized be a trade-weighted average of the exchange rates of a group of exporting countries rather than the bi-lateral exchange rates of the countries in which the U.S. imports originated. So, in addition to the use of 3- to 4-digit levels of data, the failure to examine country-specific relationships could also have led to problems with aggregation bias.

The failure of an empirical study of pass-through to examine pricing behavior across competitors also causes the exacerbation of problems with aggregation bias in terms of the product category's prices (or unit value proxies therefor). When prices/unit values (the unit value of a product is the quotient of the value of shipments divided by the quantity of shipments, i.e. simply the average (mean) price of a single unit of the product) of U.S. imports of a product from several countries are aggregated across countries, the probability of extreme heterogeneity within the product category would seem much greater than when imports from a single country are examined.

The Mann (1986) and Hooper and Mann (1989) studies also seem to confuse the pass-through issue somewhat by including questionable explanatory variables in their regression model explaining import price changes. The inclusion of foreign costs and prices of domestic substitutes as explanatory variables makes good theoretical sense. Production costs should serve as a price floor in the long-term while prices of domestic substitutes should affect demand elasticity. However, the choice of variables utilized as proxies for costs and prices of domestic substitutes points to the problematic nature of the use of such surrogates. Mann (1986) even points out the inadequacy of the proxy she chose to represent production costs of imports (the foreign consumer price index). This problem could increase the likelihood of spurious regression results.

Being mindful of the limitations of these studies caused by the above-mentioned problems, it is noteworthy that Hooper and Mann (1989) found incomplete pass-through to be the rule rather than the exception. For three of the seven U.S. imports examined the null hypothesis of zero pass-through could not be rejected. None of the significant pass-through rates was higher than twenty-eight percent (see Table 2.2 for a summary of results). These results indicated an overall unresponsiveness of prices to exchange rate changes.

Knetter (1989) examined pass-through behavior for six U.S. exports and ten German exports at the 7-digit SITC level (the data for German exports were from German sources but were equivalent to the 7-digit SITC level). While this is not as fine a level of aggregation as the 7-digit TSUSA scheme, it does ameliorate some of the problems caused by aggregation bias.

For the U.S. exports Knetter used quarterly data from 1978:1 through 1986:1 (33 observations). For the German exports he used 1977:1 through 1985:4 (36 observations). The exchange rates used were quarterly average nominal rates from the *International Financial*

Statistics Supplement on Exchange Rates. Quarterly unit-values were used as proxies for export prices.

Knetter observed that the use of industry rather than firm-level data also raises aggregation issues in those product categories where there is more than one firm involved in exporting from a particular country. He presented two scenarios under which this would not be a problem: (1) collusion leads to multiple firms acting as one firm, or (2) firms do not compete in the same export markets. Unfortunately, neither of the two scenarios he presents is likely to be common in international trade.

Knetter maintained that in those cases in which neither of these scenarios for exact aggregation exists, an assumption of the unit-value data being characteristic of the pricing behavior of an average firm is justified. While one might argue against making this assumption, the lack of time series on prices for most products makes the use of unit values necessary in almost any empirical research project examining pass-through.

An interesting feature of Knetter's work is that he apparently uses no lags of the exchange rate variable in his regression equation for measuring pass-through. Most regression based empirical studies have used at least one lagged value of the exchange rate variable.

In terms of Knetter's findings, the following seem to be important: (1) German exporters stabilized U.S. dollar prices in the U.S. market, that is pass-through for German firms exporting to the U.S. is incomplete and often very low, (2) U.S. exporters do not engage in price stabilization in foreign markets, that is they tend to engage in complete (or nearly complete) pass-through. Knetter examines several destination markets for German exports and points out that the U.S. appears to be the only one in which stabilization (incomplete pass-through) is pursued in virtually every category he examined. The finding regarding the behavior of U.S. exporters confirmed the results of other research at more aggregate levels.

Some of the specific pass-through rates (significant at the .05 level) found by Knetter for German exports to the U.S. were : (1) titanium dioxide at .15, or 15 percent, (2) small cars at .77, (3) large cars at .70, and (4)beer at .70 (to get positive pass-through rates, it was necessary to transform Knetter's reported exchange rate coefficients by adding one to their values). An interpretation of the pass-through behavior for small cars would be that approximately 77 percent of any

U.S. dollar/German Mark exchange rate change was "passed through" in the form of changes in U.S. dollar prices of small cars exported to the U.S. Expressed differently, a 10 percent increase in the value of the mark would result in a 7.7 percent increase in the dollar price of a small German car exported to the U.S.

In his concluding remarks, Knetter advanced another possible explanation for incomplete pass-through. He indicated that the "normal" practice of an exporter invoicing his products in his domestic currency is often changed for exports into the U.S.[5] due to the size of U.S. markets for many products. This pricing to the U.S. market in U.S. dollars combined with the possibility of short-run price stickiness leads to U.S. prices in dollars being fixed. This implies that pass-through will be incomplete (often zero), at least in the short-term. If prices were established in the exporter's currency and were sticky in the short-run, pass-through would be complete.

Another empirical study using disaggregated products is that of Feenstra (1989). Feenstra's major objective was to examine the issue of asymmetry of pass-through of exchange rates as compared to those for tariffs, that is whether tariff changes were passed-through differently from exchange rate changes.

Feenstra examined three U.S. imports from Japan that were disaggregated to an approximation of the 7-digit SITC level. The products were large motorcycles, automobiles(in the SITC scheme, there is one category for automobiles while in the TSUSA scheme there are three: four cylinders and less, over four but not more than six cylinders, and more than six cylinders), and compact trucks. The data were quarterly and Feenstra's sample period was 1978:1 through 1984:4 (28 observations) for motorcycles; 1974:1 through 1981:1 (29 observations) for automobiles; and 1977:1 through 1987:1 (41 observations) for compact trucks. His import price data came from the U.S. Department of Commerce, Bureau of the Census. Feenstra did not identify the source of his exchange rate data but did indicate that he was using an average of the contemporaneous and first lag of quarterly exchange rates. He indicated that this would make the variable something of an "expected" exchange rate to which importers would respond.

Feenstra's regression equation included explanatory variables other than the exchange rate and its lags. For example, he included a proxy for foreign factor prices (Japanese domestic wholesale prices for each product intended as a surrogate for production costs), a proxy for income (total U.S. expenditure on each product through an instrumental variable), and a proxy for the price of a domestic substitute (U.S. consumer prices or the U.S. price of steel). These proxies might cause concern for some researchers and lead them to question the study's results. Feenstra also mixed different levels of aggregation with some variables being used at a 2-digit level (e.g., some of the U.S. consumer prices) while others are used at a 7-digit level (e.g., unit values for the three products).

Feenstra imposed a second-degree polynomial constraint on the distributed lag structure of the exchange rate variable. He stated that the erratic behavior of the coefficients in his regression equations was a major factor in his decision to impose this constraint on the lag structure. Some researchers question the validity of this rationale for the imposition of such a constraint. In a telephone conversation with the present author in April of 1990, Will Melick of the Federal Reserve System maintained that the use of such a constraint could conceal other problems inherent in the data (such as serial correlation) that could be dealt with in some other, more statistically appropriate, fashion.

However, Feenstra also reported that his results from unconstrained regressions that were run in an attempt to help determine the appropriate lag length for the exchange rate variable were not significantly different from the constrained model. He did not report the actual results of this unconstrained model. His observation that the pass-through of the exchange rate changes was quite rapid (the exchange rate coefficient estimates had become virtually zero by the second or third lag) held true with both the constrained and unconstrained versions of the regression model.

Feenstra also utilized a geometric constraint in a final model. He imposed this constraint by including two lagged values of the dependent variable as explanatory variables. The pass-through rates for this geometric lag model were very similar to those reported for the second-degree polynomial model.

While Feenstra's research had some shortcomings (in addition to the shortcomings mentioned above, Feenstra observed that the coefficients of the exchange rate variable and its lags should be interpreted with caution as he did not detrend his data), he did some things that added strength to it. One strength of the study is the above-mentioned fact that Feenstra estimated several alternative specifications of the regression equation. He also estimated the regressions over various sub-periods to determine if there were changes in pass-through behavior from one period to another.

Feenstra's major findings were: (1) there is symmetry of pass-through of exchange rates and tariffs, which implies that the response of import prices to exchange rates might predict the effect of changes in tariffs, (2) there is symmetry of pass-through of exchange rate changes in periods of appreciation and depreciation, and (3) the variation in results across industries means that additional empirical evidence is needed before any sort of generalizations regarding pass-through behavior are made.

The final empirical study to be reviewed in detail is that of Marston (1989) examining Japanese exports. One of the interesting features of this study is the use of monthly data. Marston also examined seventeen different products, which is the largest number of products in any of the studies reviewed here.

Marston's price data were gathered from the Bank of Japan and approximate data at the 5- to 7-digit SITC level. He uses the export shares of each product to calculate a weighted average exchange rate variable based on the exchange rates of the major importers of the product. This means that he cannot determine if there are differences in pass-through behavior across countries as all importing countries are treated as one. The explanatory variable whose coefficient can be interpreted as a pass-through rate is termed by Marston as a "pricing to market" variable and is different from any variable contained in earlier studies (pass-through is calculated as one minus the coefficient of Marston's PTM variable).

Marston used 95 monthly observations in his log-log OLS regression. All variables were expressed as first differences of their log values to ameliorate problems with spurious correlation between variables. Marston did include explanatory variables other than the pass-through variables (e.g. foreign (non-Japanese) industrial production).

A complete summary of pass-through rates is provided in Table 2.2, but Marston concluded that profit margins are varied systematically as Japanese exporters price to their foreign markets. He also concluded that pass-through behavior is symmetric for exchange rate appreciations and depreciations. However, he found some support for lower levels of pass-through by Japanese producers when the yen is appreciating. This was the case for five of the seventeen products examined, although two of these five demonstrated very marginal support for asymmetrical behavior.

Table 2.2

Summary of Import Pass-Through Rates for Studies Reviewed

Study	Exporting Country(ies)	Destination Country(ies)	Sample Period	# of obs.
Dunn (1970)	Canada U.S.	Canada U.S.	1950-62 semi-ann.	17 - 22
USITC (1983)	Japan W. Ger.	U.S.	1977-82 quarterly	24
Kreinin, et al (1987)	Japan W. Ger. U.K.	U.S.	Mid 70's- early 80's	Cross- Sect.
Knetter (1988)	W. Ger.	U.S.	1977-85 quarterly	36
Hooper & Mann (1989)	Pool of Large Exporters	U.S.	1977-86 quarterly	40
Feenstra (1989)	Japan	U.S.	1974-81 car 1977-87 truck 1978-84 cycle all quarterly	29 41 28
Marston (1989)	Japan	Pool of Countries	1980-87 monthly	95

Table 2.2. (Continued)

Study	Level of Data	PT Model(s)	Products Examined	PT%
Dunn	Approximate 3- to 4-digit SIC	OLS, one lag of FX, no ind. var. other than FX	Window Glass Gasoline Crude Oil Rolled Steel Copper Coal	#
USITC	Approximate 5- to 6-di. TSUSA	Log-log OLS, 2nd deg. PDL, corrected for autocorr., 2 to 7 FX lags, other in.var.	Piano:Japan Piano:Ger. Brass:Japan Brass:Ger. Bicy.:Japan	39 59[**] 27 -43 -45
Kreinin, et al	4-digit SIC	Log-nor. OLS, crs.-sec. data, other in. var., PT is dep. var.	NR	NR
Knetter	German equivalent of 7-digit SITC	Log-log OLS with country effect, no FX lags	Tit. Diox. Small Cars Large Cars Beer White Wine Spark. Wine Potas. Chl. Mining Wax Fan Belts Motorcycles	15 77 70 70 59 56 10 6 -37 85[**]
Hooper & Mann	3- to 4-digit SIC	Log-log OLS, 2nd deg. PDL, other in. var. Also unconstrained lag. # of FX lags not reported.	Textiles Footwear Const. Mch. Frt. & Veg. Apparel Steel Pulp Mill	28 18 28 14 -6[**] -2[**] 96[**]

Table 2.2. (Continued)

Study	Level of Data	PT Model(s)	Products Examined	PT%
Feenstra	Approximate 7-digit SITC	Log-log OLS, 2nd deg. PDL, 4 lags of FX, other in. var. Also: Geometric lag and unconstrained lag.	2nd deg. PDL	
			Cars	71
			Trucks	63
			Cycles	89
			Geometric	
			Cars	96
			Trucks	45
			Cycles	40**
Marston	Approximate 5- to 7-dig. SITC	Log-log OLS, all var. 1st-diff., zero to 3 FX lags, other in. var.	Color TV's	35
			Tape Recd.	5
			Tape Decks	41
			Record Pl.	10
			Amplifiers	-11
			Rec. Tape	13
			Microwaves	72
			Cameras	92**
			Copiers	49
			Small Cars	48
			Cars	11
			Sm. Trucks	93**
			Trucks	59
			Motorcyles	48
			Tires & Tb.	-6
			Ag. Trac.	51
			Const. Tr.	15

*Not statistically sig. at .05 level.

**Not statistically sig. at .10 level.

NR = Not Reported

= Coefficients not interpretable as PT rates. None of the simple correlations was sig. at the .10 level.

Brief mention will be made of a study by Gagnon and Knetter (1990). The data utilized apparently approximate the 7-digit SITC level on automobiles. However, the fact that only twelve annual observations are utilized makes any of the results highly questionable. These results are not reported here due to the small number of observations and the incumbent danger involved in reaching conclusions from the use of such questionable statistics.

SUMMARY

A point on the usefulness of previous empirical research on pass-through should be mentioned. Kenen and Pack (1980) observed, "the evidence . . . is rather hard to integrate, because studies of exchange rates and price levels use a variety of exchange rate and price data. They use different weighting schemes to generate their indexes of effective exchange rates - bilateral weights, global weights, and multilateral weights. They use different data on domestic prices . . . " In addition to the differences in types of data there are also differences in the types of models utilized to measure pass-through and in the construction of the variables whose coefficients are to be interpreted as the "pass-through" rate. These differences in approach create a great deal of confusion and make cross-study comparisons practically impossible. With these difficulties in mind, Table 2.2 was constructed in an attempt to summarize the findings of those empirical studies reviewed above from the era of floating exchange rates in which disaggregated data were used.

The confusion caused by different approaches to empirical pass-through research is exemplified by comparing comments found in two studies. Kenen and Pack (1980) note that, "These choices [of level and type of data to use] have important consequences. Consider, for example, the results obtained by Hooper and Lowrey (1979). Using global trade weights to measure the effective exchange rate for the U.S. dollar, they find . . . the . . . pass-through . . . was less than complete. Using bilateral weights, however, they find that . . . the pass-through was virtually complete."

Compare the Kenen and Pack comment to one by Hooper and Mann (1989): " . . . disaggregating the data appears to reduce total pass-through and reduce the length of the lags. This . . . highlights the importance of the choice, construction, and aggregation of . . . data [used] to analyze pass-through." While Kenen and Pack cited a study showing that disaggregated data produced higher rates of pass-through, Hooper and Mann indicate just the opposite.

The State of Pass-Through Research: Conceptual

The number of empirical research studies that have demonstrated that pass-through behavior does not occur as might be predicted under the law of one price is substantial. This has led to the development of several conceptual ideas that might explain observed instances of incomplete pass-through.

Krugman (1987a) reviews several of these explanations and offers his favored version, which he terms as "pricing to market." The basic contention is that market conditions in an exporter's markets will determine his pricing behavior. This will often lead to incomplete pass-through. Krugman's and other theoretical explanations of incomplete pass-through are grounded in the imperfectly competitive markets model and owe their origins to the field of industrial organization. Until the basic concepts of industrial organization were outlined, the sort of international price discrimination that results from incomplete pass-through would have been deemed impossible under the perfectly competitive markets model (even though as shown above, incomplete pass-through can be explained within the context of the perfect competition model). As Krugman (1987a) advocates, it is time for these recently developed hypotheses to be empirically tested.

The State of Pass-Through Research: Empirical

Most extant empirical research into the pass-through phenomenon was conducted using such highly aggregated data that its value to a manager is limited. Some of the small number of studies using more disaggregated data still have problems with aggregation bias (using 3- or 4-digit data) and the use of multi-lateral exchange rates. These problems limit the usefulness of even these studies to the manager concerned with the pricing behavior of specific international competitors.

Previous empirical studies have almost universally excluded developing countries. This is somewhat troubling in an economy-wide study but is extremely so for firm-level studies. It is not at all unusual for a developing country such as Korea to be the major exporter of certain products to the United States. If such a country is systematically excluded from consideration in pass-through studies, the conclusions of such studies would seem tenuous at best.

Finally, the sample size of products in previous empirical studies of pass-through has normally been very small. As can be seen from Table 2.2, the greatest number of products to be examined in a single study was seventeen. Most of the studies examine fewer than five products. Once again, this is cause for concern when generalizability of the results is at issue.

When the above-mentioned shortcomings of existing empirical studies are considered it becomes obvious that additional research into the pass-through phenomenon is needed. An observation made by Herd (1987) seems appropriate: "The issue as to whether there is . . . pass-through of exchange rate movements to import prices is still open in the literature."

NOTES

1. For a concise history of exchange rate regimes from 1870 to present see U.S. International Trade Commission, *Floating Exchange Rates and U.S. Competitiveness*, publication #1332, December 1982.

2. See Isard, Peter, "How Far Can We Push the 'Law of One Price?'" *American Economic Review*, vol. 67, pp. 942-948 and Kravis, Irving B. and Robert E. Lipsey, "Price Behavior in the Light of Balance of Payments Theories," *Journal of International Economics*, 1978, pp. 193-246 for detailed studies of the failure of the law of one price to hold for different types of products.

3. From Devine, P.J., et al, *An Introduction to Industrial Economics*, 4th edition, 1985.

4. For reviews of these studies, see Herd, Richard, *Import and Export Price Equations for Manufactures*, working paper #43, Organization for Economic Cooperation and Development, Department of Economics and Statistics, Balance of Payments Division, June 1987 and Goldstein, M. and M.S. Khan, "Income and Price Effects in Foreign Trade," in Ronald W. Jones and Peter B. Kenen, eds., *Handbook of International Economics*, volume II, North-Holland, New York, 1985, among others.

5. See Hamada, Koichi and Akiyoshi Horiuchi, "Monetary, Financial and Real Effects of Yen Internationalization," in J. David Richardson and Sven Arndt, eds., *Real Financial Linkages Among Open Economies*, MIT Press, Cambridge, 1987, pp. 167-192 and McKinnon, Ronald, *Money in International Exchange*, New York, Oxford University Press, 1979, chapter 4 for some observations on the prevalence of dollar-based invoicing of U.S. imports.

III
Research Issues and Questions

This chapter discusses the issues and questions to be addressed by the present research. The trade policy issues that are related to the research are considered, the firm-level policy issues that could be impacted by the firm's response to exchange rate fluctuations are discussed, the relationship between the concepts of pass-through and pricing to market (PTM) is examined, and the key research questions to be explored are further expounded.

EFFECTS OF EXPLORATORY NATURE
OF THE RESEARCH

Aaker and Day (1986) comment that, "Exploratory research is used when one is seeking insights into the general nature of a problem, the possible decision alternatives, and relevant variables that need to be considered. There is typically little prior knowledge upon which to build." They continue by saying that, " . . . the researcher begins without firm preconceptions as what will be found." Since this study will ask the most basic question of whether exchange rate changes are passed through to import prices it would seem that the above observations describing some of the characteristics of exploratory studies would be applicable.

Aaker and Day (1986) also mention that, "Exploratory research hypotheses are either vague and ill-defined or do not exist at all." They even cite an example in which the, " . . . hypothesis is extremely tentative and provides at best only a partial answer to the research question. Exploratory research is also useful for establishing priorities among research questions and for learning about the practical problems of carrying out the research." As will be seen below, many of these observations are also appropriate to the present study. Learning the "right" questions to ask and the problems inherent in investigating them are both important objectives of this study.

POLICY AND THEORY ISSUES
AT THE MACRO-LEVEL

The principal purpose of this research is to determine whether exchange rate fluctuations are passed-through to import prices in the U.S. market. The empirical results of the study in regards to this question will have implications for the debate on U.S. government policy concerning trade issues and should also contribute toward the development of international pricing theory.

If the results indicate that exchange rate changes are followed by proportional (or nearly so) changes in the prices of U.S. imports they would tend to refute charges of dumping by foreign producers. This finding would also tend to support the grounding of international pricing theory in a perfectly competitive markets model with its incumbent concept of the law of one price.

Should the results indicate that pass-through rates are low or, at the extreme, zero (indicating some degree of pricing to market), the issue of dumping and other unfair trading practices by foreign competitors would come to the fore. Such a verification of international price discrimination would also lend support to calls for the grounding of international pricing theory in a model that assumes some form of imperfectly competitive markets.

POLICY ISSUES AT THE FIRM LEVEL

One of the principal elements of the value-added of the research is that the relationship between import price changes and exchange rate changes will be examined at the finest level of aggregation possible when utilizing readily available data sources. The use of such micro-level data will shift the emphasis of the study to the level of the firm and make the study useful to international marketers as they determine their pricing strategies, especially in the U.S. market.

If the results indicate that PTM is the prevalent pricing behavior for foreign firms inporting into the U.S. market, the prescriptive behavior for both U.S. and foreign participants in that market might involve such actions as cost reduction efforts (e.g., changing sources of inputs) or even abandonment of the market. If such behavior can be empirically verified in the U.S. market, decisions as to how to best compete can be made from a more knowledgeable perspective. A firm's expectations of competitive behavior based on its knowledge of such factors as industry structure in a given market might not be reflective of reality. Knowledge-based competitive decisions should prove to be superior to basing such decisions on hunches.

PASS-THROUGH, PTM, AND THE NEED FOR FURTHER RESEARCH

It seems clear from the review of relevant literature that the question as to whether and how pass-through occurs is at best only partially addressed by existing empirical research. This state of affairs has also led to confusion in the development of theoretical explanations of pricing behavior in an international context.

If incomplete pass-through can be empirically verified for a large sample of disaggregated products this would tend to support Krugman's (1987) contentions regarding PTM behavior. If PTM were adhered to in the pricing of a specific import into a large country such as the U.S., the result could well be an extremely low pass-through rate (assuming that such a good is treated independently so that price changes by an exporter to the U.S. are not in response to a change in the general price level in the U.S. market). This means that the dollar price of a specific import might not respond to a change in exchange rates because the pricing strategy being utilized for the product is market-based rather than cost-based. There can be little doubt that a non-U.S. firm's marginal cost is affected by changes in exchange rates but the firm's response to such a change in costs is still an empirical question. There is certainly a need for such research at the firm-level.

KEY RESEARCH QUESTIONS

As previously discussed, the overriding issue to be examined in this study is whether U.S. import prices (expressed in U.S. dollars) respond to fluctuations in bi-lateral exchange rates. One would assume that if a pricing strategy were cost-based then import prices would be adjusted to reflect changes in exchange rates. However, if a more market-oriented pricing strategy were to be pursued one would suspect that import prices might not reflect (at least fully reflect) changes in exchange rates, or as Krugman (1987) termed it, PTM would occur. The degree to which PTM does actually occur in particular markets will be addressed in this study.

An issue that can be explored simultaneously is whether there is some time lag for responses of import prices to changes in exchange rates (assuming that there is a response). The decision process that is followed as foreign producers deliberate on their pricing response to exchange rate fluctuations can be examined through the use of high frequency (such as monthly) time series data on import prices and exchange rates. These producers face a great deal of uncertainty when trying to decide when and to what extent such responses should be made.

Other conditions that could impact pass-through behavior can also be examined to determine their impact on pricing responses to exchange rate changes. It seems possible that pass-through behavior could be country-specific. Charges that some countries, such as Japan, target critical industries for export development through their national industrial policies could be examined to some extent when exploring PTM behavior. If it seems that a particular country systematically engages in PTM behavior it would serve as an indictment of that country in this regard. If such country-specific activity were found to also be specific to certain products (e.g., high growth industries), this charge of targeting would be even stronger.

Products can also be examined by product type, or class, to determine if empirical regularities appear in pricing behavior according to such types. Products could be classified as: (1) consumer durables, (2) consumer non-durables, (3) intermediate goods (e.g., component parts, supplies, etc.), or (4) capital goods. If pass-through behavior is systematically different across one or more of these product types this could also shed some light on the reasons for differences in such behavior. For example, those products that are more amenable to differentiation might demonstrate pass-through behaviors that are substantially different from those sold in commodity-like market settings.

Import price and exchange rate data series might also be broken down into periods of exchange rate depreciation and appreciation to determine whether pass-through behavior is symmetric. If such behavior were asymmetric then it would differ in periods of exchange rate depreciation and appreciation. If a foreign producer were to pass-through an appreciation of his currency the result would be higher dollar prices in the U.S. market. Some producers might be reticent to do so. However, they might want to pass-through a depreciation of their currency in the form of lower dollar prices in order to increase their U.S. market share.

If a wide range of pass-through rates were observed additional questions could be contemplated. These might include an examination of the impact that market structure or strategic marketing concepts (e.g., market share or market growth rate) might have on pass-through behavior. However, for those questions other than the basic issue of whether pass-through occurs at all to be examined satisfactorily would require that a fairly large number of the products being studied demonstrate some level of pass-through. If the prices of a great majority of the products studied do not respond to exhange rate changes the additional questions lose their importance to a great extent.

IV

Research Method: Sample Design

TIME FRAME OF THE SAMPLE

The time period to be analyzed is January of 1979 through December of 1988 (data were available for 1978 but the use of 12 monthly lags of the exchange rate variable effectively makes January 1979 the initial observation). Some reasons for choosing this period are: (1) exchange rates of most major U.S. trading partners were floating, (2) the dollar experienced three distinct cycles against most major currencies, and (3) many important traded products, such as certain types of electronics, were not produced in earlier time periods.

DATA ON IMPORT PRICES

The ideal data on U.S. import prices for a project examining pricing practices at a micro level would consist of prices collected directly from firms in the various industries of interest. This primary data collection could be handled in such a manner as to eliminate many of the problems created when secondary data are utilized in such a micro study. As will be discussed further below, problems such as heterogeneity of products that are contained within the same product category of the various classification schemes commonly utilized for the reporting of data on international trade could be practically elimated. Collection of this sort of primary data would greatly ameliorate the problems inherent in the necessity of the use of unit values as proxies for actual product prices. However, this sort of data collection is simply not feasible from either an economic or temporal standpoint. This necessitates the use of secondary data sources.

There are two agencies that collect large amounts of data on U.S. trade statistics: (1) the United Nations collects trade data for almost all nations of the world, and (2) the U.S. Customs Service collects U.S. import and export data that are processed by the Bureau of the Census (a branch of the U.S. Department of Commerce). The Customs Service collects import and export declaration documents and forwards them to the Census Bureau for processing.

U.N. data are collected from the governments of its member nations. This means that all U.N. data on U.S. imports are also generated from the data originally collected by the U.S. Customs Service. The original source of all U.S. import data is then the U.S. Customs Service.

When the Bureau of the Census processes the import data provided it by the Customs Service the imported products have been classified into one of approximately 16,000 seven-digit commodity categories (this 7-digit system was changed to a 10-digit system in 1989). This product classification scheme is commonly referred to as the TSUSA (Tariff Schedule of the United States Annotated) scheme.

The decision as to which of these 16,000-plus product categories an imported product should be contained in is made by the importer when he completes a declaration document. The appropriateness of the classification is verified by the Customs Service. The information gathered from each declaration document includes the U.S. dollar value (for import values reported in foreign currencies the Customs Service utilizes the exchange rate on the date of departure of the product from the foreign port to translate its value into a dollar value) and quantity of a product shipment along with the country of origin. The principal reason that there are so many more TSUSA classifications at the 7-digit level than there are in the 7-digit level of other classification schemes (e.g., around 3,000 in the SITC scheme) is that many of the import duties imposed by the U.S. are different for products that have only slight differences. For example, in the United Nations' Standard International Trade Classification (SITC) scheme one of the 7-digit classifications is color TV's. In the TSUSA scheme there are seven different classifications of color TV's and each of these can be subject to a different level of import duty.

Any U.S. import data reported in a classification scheme other than TSUSA are simply rearrangements of TSUSA data (often aggregations of several TSUSA numbers into one number in another scheme). This includes the U.N.'s SITC and ISIC (International Standard Industrial Classification) schemes as well as the various schemes, such as SIC (Standard Industrial Classification), utilized by U.S. government entities.

Research concerning pricing behavior at micro levels that must rely on secondary data sources would seem likely to benefit from the use of the most disaggregated secondary data available. The more disaggregated the data are, the less likely that the composition of the products in any given product category will be extremely heterogeneous. Greater homogeneity within a product category will cause the unit value of the category to be a more representative proxy of the product's price.

The finest level of disaggregation of TSUSA data (the 7-digit level) is finer than the finest level of disaggregation of any of the other classification schemes. TSUSA data are also available in monthly series while some of the other classification schemes are reported on a quarterly basis. Finally, since all other data schemes are rearrangements of the TSUSA scheme, and therefore subject to problems such as a lack of a true one-to-one correspondence with the TSUSA scheme and errors in transcription, it seems that the use of the original monthly, 7-digit TSUSA data is advisable in the present study.

The method used in collecting TSUSA data lends another strength to their use in the present study. One concern that any researcher examining import prices would need to address is the problem of international transfer pricing. This situation arises when intrafirm transfers of products are made across international borders. If a transaction is not "arms length" in nature, there would always exist the possibility that the product value reported to government authorities is not a true market value. This misreporting could take place in an effort to avoid import duties, reduce income tax liabilities, etc. However, the U.S. Customs Service utilizes both computerized and non-computerized methods to prevent this sort of distortion of prices from occurring.

The Customs Service has a computer program that gives immediate feedback to a customs inspector as to the true market value of some products. If the importer claims a value that is outside a rather narrow band of "acceptable" unit values for that product the inspector is alerted to the discrepancy and can require detailed documentation to verify the reported value. The Customs inspector can challenge both prices that are considered too low and too high.

An importer might report a price lower than the actual transaction price in order to reduce the amount of import duty. He might report a price higher than the actual transaction price in order to avoid the imposition of higher import duties or to qualify for a lower rate of duty. For example, some Japanese steel manufacturers have been known to report inflated prices in order to avoid the imposition of the so-called "trigger price" mechanism. If Japanese steel imported into the U.S. falls below a certain price an additional import duty is "triggered." Using a scheme of artificial price inflation, the Japanese importer invoices his U.S. customer for a price high enough to avoid the imposition of the higher duty. He later rebates the overcharge to the U.S. customer in some fashion.

It is also possible that inflated prices could be reported in order to qualify for lower rates of import duties. For example, if the duty percentage for a product category is ten percent when the unit price is below $5.00 while the duty percentage for this product category is eight percent when the unit price is $5.00 or more, it is in the financial best-interest of the importer to inflate his transaction price. The net result would be a lower import duty (e.g., $4.85 * .10 = $.485 in duty while $5.10 * .08 = $.408 in duty).

For those products that are not yet incorporated into this computerized data base the customs inspector can contact a National Import Specialist at the National Office of the Customs Service in New York City. This national specialist can provide data on market value for any of the over 16,000 TSUSA categories. This sort of verification process protects the integrity of the unit value information provided by the Customs Service.

A final consideration in the choice of classification schemes was the potential for problems being created by having a wide range of composition of products within a single product category. This problem of heterogeneity will still exist in TSUSA categories but is somewhat ameliorated by the fineness with which products are broken down under TSUSA. For example, when a unit value is calculated for a color television one would not be averaging a "big-screen" television with a 9-inch portable if TSUSA data, rather than SITC data, were being used. This should make the unit values calculated using TSUSA data a somewhat more representative proxy for price than would be the case under other trade classification schemes. However, this heterogeneity problem is somewhat exacerbated by the fact that the available data forces all firms in an industry in a particular country to be treated as if they were one company.

These data were obtained from their final repository at the U.S. Department of Commerce. They were retrieved electronically through a field office of the Commerce Department. Non-electronic means of data collection for a data set that would be as large as the one necessary for the present study would consume inordinate amounts of time.

DESIRABLE FEATURES OF THE
SAMPLE OF IMPORT PRICES

In research utilizing time series data it is desirable that data for all variables cover the same time period. Higher frequency data are also desirable as they can lead to a greater number of observations, thus increasing degrees of freedom in statistical tests, and to a greater likelihood that a firm's responses to changes are more readily identifiable.

Availability of high frequency data are assured by the use of TSUSA data, which are reported on a monthly basis. However, availability of continuous time series is often problematic when secondary data are utilized and 7-digit TSUSA data are definitely susceptible to this problem (problems of non-continuous time series refer to series that have many months or even years of consecutive observations missing due to changes in TSUSA numbers or introductions of completely new products, not to situations where an occasional monthly observation is missing). In fact, the proliferation of new TSUSA categories in the 1970's and early 1980's due to the creation of more complex trade rules for imports exacerbated this problem.

This proliferation of product categories made it necessary in 1984 for the Customs Service to begin recycling TSUSA numbers almost immediately upon the changing of a particular product category's number. Such changing of numbers is necessitated by the splitting of a product category into two or more sub-categories or by the combination of product categories into one number. The only way to assure that electronically retrieved data are indeed a part of a continuous time series is to limit the time series to those that utilized the same TSUSA number throughout the entire time period of the study.

This concern with assuring that continuous time series for a product category be maintained throughout the time period of the sample led to the imposition of the requirement that for a 7-digit TSUSA number to be included in the sample it must have been in continuous use for the entire period to be examined. As will be discussed further below, under certain conditions this requirement had to be waived in order to retain certain desirable characteristics (such as a sufficient number of capital goods) in the final sample.

An additional characteristic of the sample that was felt desirable is that the products to be included should be sold in markets not dominated by one seller. Since some authors have argued that market structure would have an impact on pass-through behavior (even though Kreinin, et al (1987) found that it did not), it was felt that if the extreme of monopoly were controlled for the potential for a confounding effect being exerted by market stucture considerations would be considerably reduced.

A necessary characteristic of the sample is that the data on the products be reported in such a way that unit values can be calculated. Both the value and quantity of imports of a product must be reported in order for these average prices to be calculated and utilized as proxies for actual product prices. Unfortunately, the quantity of imports of some product categories is not reported by the Bureau of the Census. Such categories cannot be included in the sample to be examined. For example, TSUSA number 6622065, which contains machines for cleaning and filling containers, could not be included in the sample for this reason. Fortunately, this omission of quantity is not a common occurrence.

Another desirable characteristic of the sample is that the products to be included are important in the overall scheme of U.S. trade. This would require that the total value of imports of a product be rather large. This would also lead to the overall sample containing a substantial percentage of total U.S. imports.

CRITERIA FOR IMPORT
PRICE SAMPLE SELECTION

With these broader characteristics in mind, the specific criteria to be utilized in the selection of the sample were developed. The initial decision rule related to the desire to have products included that were important in terms of overall value of trade. The rule was that for a product category to be considered for inclusion in the sample its total volume of imports in 1988 had to exceed $75 million. The rule was somewhat arbitrary in nature but was similar to that used in the USITC (1983) study in which the cutoff was $100 million. A computer search was conducted through the U.S. Department of Commerce using this initial cutoff point and the number of TSUSA categories to be considered for inclusion in the sample was reduced from over 16,000 to 874. These 874 categories comprised approximately 79 percent of total U.S. imports for 1988 (see Table 4.1).

The second decision rule to be applied was the one requiring that the time series for a product category be continuous from January 1979 through December 1988. To verify that a product category had been constantly carried under a single 7-digit TSUSA number for the

Table 4.1
U.S. Trade Data - 1988 Imports for Consumption:
Customs Value

Total Value of Imports	Total Number of Items Exceeding $75 million	Total Value of Items Exceeding $75 million
$437,140,185,000	874	$345,765,280,000

Source: Customized Computer Run from U.S. Dept. of Commerce

entire time period the initial computer run from the Commerce Department contained the annual value of trade under the reported TSUSA number for both 1988 and 1979. If the reported value for 1979 was zero this meant that this TSUSA number was not being used during the initial time period of the sample.

Appendix A is a complete listing of the 7-digit TSUSA categories resulting from the Commerce Department computer run. Each of these categories (874 in total) had total import values during 1988 of at least $75 million. However, many of the numbers listed in the appendix showed a value of zero in 1979. This means that the TSUSA number either changed between 1979 and 1988 or that the product was not being imported into the U.S. in 1979. For this group of heavily imported products it seems likely that most were being imported in 1979. The probable reason for the zero value was that the product was being reported under a different number in that year. The rule of eliminating TSUSA numbers showing a zero value in 1979 deleted 503 of the 874 categories exceeding $75 million.

A desire to focus on manufactures with their incumbent higher levels of value-added led to an examination of the broad TSUSA categories in anticipation of the possible elimination of such categories. Table 4.2 contains a brief description of the broad TSUSA categories at the highest level of aggregation (one-digit).

Table 4.2
Description of One-digit TSUSA Categories

Schedule 1 - Animal and Vegatable Products
Schedule 2 - Wood and Paper, Printed Matter
Schedule 3 - Textile Fibers and Textile Products
Schedule 4 - Chemicals and Related Products
Schedule 5 - Nonmetallic Minerals and Products
Schedule 6 - Metals and Metal Products
Schedule 7 - Specified Products, Miscellaneous and Non-
                  enumerated Products
Schedule 8 - Special Classification Provisions

Source: *Understanding United States Foreign Trade Data*,
International Trade Admin., U.S. Dept. of Commerce, August 1985.

Since Schedules 1 and 2 appeared to be comprised substantially of commodity-type products, an initial decision rule was utilized under which all TSUSA numbers beginning in 1 or 2 were eliminated from consideration (this elminated 78 numbers not already eliminated). In addition, all crude oil and derivatives thereof utilized for energy production were excluded. This additional elimination of products sold in a commodity-like environment removed only 13 TSUSA numbers not previously eliminated but these numbers accounted for almost 10 percent of the total value of imports in 1988.

One of the most severe limitations of international trade data is the heterogeneity of products that fall within a particular classification. As explained above, this was the principal reason for choosing the TSUSA classification scheme over other schemes, such as SITC. However, even the TSUSA classification scheme is not perfect in this regard. The quest for maximization of homogeneity within product categories led to additional TSUSA numbers being eliminated from consideration for inclusion in the present sample.

One relatively simple method for eliminating products with excessive heterogeneity is to examine the TSUSA product titles. For example, if a product category is identified as "aluminum sheets and strips not specifically provided for (nspf)," this serves as a warning that this is the product classification into which all previously unclassified aluminum sheets and strips are placed. This will likely result in a mixture of very different types of aluminum products whose values would vary widely. This would cause drastic swings in unit values that are completely independent of changes in exchange rates.

This type of heterogeneity needs to be eliminated from the sample to whatever extent possible. In addition to the products whose TSUSA titles included the nspf label, those products whose titles included the "not elsewhere specified (nes)" label (e.g., nitriles nes), the term "etc." (e.g., magnetic vises, brakes, etc.), or the term "other" (e.g., other brake parts for motor vehicles) were eliminated from consideration at this point in the sample selection process due to the likelihood that they would be extremely heterogeneous in composition.

Certain TSUSA numbers contained a product and "parts" of that product (e.g., parts of video games). It seems likely that including parts of a product in the same category as the completely assembled final product would cause severe heterogeneity within that category. Product categories containing the term "parts" were therefore eliminated from consideration for inclusion in the final sample.

Another problem with some TSUSA categories is that they consist of products whose quantities are expressed in different quantity measures at different times or by different importers. For example, the quantity of screws might be expressed in terms of weight by some importers while others would express the quantity in terms of the number of screws. When this situation occurs, the Census Bureau does not report any measure of quantity. Since a report of the quantity of an import must be utilized in computing its unit value, those products for which no quantity was available were eliminated from the sample. Only ten numbers that had not been previously removed were eliminated due to this problem.

In order to control for the possible effects of market structure on pass-through and to avoid the inclusion of an industry with a monopolistic market structure it was decided that product categories in which more than 95 percent of total U.S. imports were accounted for by one country would be removed from consideration. This only affected two product categories that had not been eliminated by other decision rules.

After the above decision rules for inclusion in the sample were applied, the remaining TSUSA categories were examined in greater detail. Since one of the potential explanators of pass-through behavior was believed to be the product type (consumer durable, consumer durable, intermediate good, or capital good), an effort was made to include approximately equal numbers of each product type. It was also decided that for statistical significance reasons pertaining to sample size, it would be appropriate for each product type to be represented by about thirty different TSUSA product categories. The desire to have this number of products from each of the four product types led to the necessity of using subjective judgements in breaking some of the above-listed decision rules. The previously applied decision rule filters had reduced the 874 product categories with imports of $75 million or more in 1988 down to only 98 with 22 of these being classified as consumer durables, 17 consumer non-durables, 42 intermediate goods, and 17 capital goods. It is obvious that making the decision rules conditional was necessary in order to achieve the inclusion of thirty TSUSA numbers within each of the four product types.

The first rule to be set aside was that of a continuous time series. Since the reason for discontinuity of the series in some cases was nothing more than a renumbering of TSUSA categories that was dictated by legislative changes in import duties, it was decided that those series with substantial import activity (defined as 1988 import volume exceeding $200 million) would be reexamined to determine whether it was practical to construct a continuous time series by checking the previously used TSUSA number and updating the series. An example of a product included in the final sample as a result of this examination was TSUSA number 6921014 for four-cylinder automobiles. This category accounted for almost five percent of total imports in 1988. The total number of product categories added to the sample by violating this continuous time series decision was 38.

The product type that presented the greatest challenge in terms of locating thirty TSUSA numbers that would fall under its rubric was consumer non-durables. This led to the selective violation of the rule to eliminate all TSUSA numbers from schedules one and two. The end result was that two numbers from schedule one and two from schedule two were added to the final sample.

This reexamination of the products in schedule one (animal and vegetable products) also led to the recognition that some TSUSA numbers representing substantial volumes of imports had been excluded from consideration due to the inclusion of such terms as "etc." and "not specifically provided for" in their descriptions. The decision was made to review all such numbers whose import volume exceeded $200 million in 1988.

A good example of this situation is TSUSA number 1670515 which accounted for over $800 million in imports in 1988. Upon closer examination, it was determined that this category, entitled "beer, ale, etc. in glass containers not over one gallon in size," was really quite homogeneous and consisted almost entirely of beer in glass bottles that contained 12 ounces. Another example of this situation was found in a category entitled "nuts of iron or steel, not specifically provided for." This number accounted for a large import volume and was found to demonstrate a unit-value behavior that indicated that the category was either relatively homogeneous or that the product mix that comprised the category remained relatively constant during the period of the sample. In either case, the result was a well-behaved unit-value series that seemd to be a fair representation of the actual pricing behavior for that product. This selective violation of the decision rule led to the inclusion of nine numbers that had previously been excluded.

One final method for determining whether heterogeneity was a serious problem was to manually observe the unit value time series in an effort to discover erratic behavior in the series. If prices/unit values demonstrated this sort of erratic pattern the series was eliminated from the sample. A closer examination of the 149 seven-digit numbers that were still possibilities at this point (874 numbers reduced to 98 after applying all decision rules, 38 added by selective inclusion of previously incomplete time series, 4 added by selective inclusion of products from schedules one and two, and 9 added by selective inclusion of products whose descriptions contained terms such as "etc.") revealed that 12 of these products demonstrated extreme fluctuations in unit values and should be eliminated from further consideration because of this high degree of heterogeneity within the category.

The net result was the selection of an initial sample of 137 seven-digit TSUSA product categories. This sample included 34 products classified as consumer durables, 34 consumer non-durables, 32 capital goods and 37 intermediate goods (e.g., industrial inputs and business supplies). It was felt that having in excess of thirty categories within each product type would provide a safety stock in the event that closer examination of the categories revealed that additional categories needed to be excluded from the sample. It should also be noted that the decisions as to which TSUSA categories should be included in each of the four product types is based on the subjective judgement of the author and is, of course, subject to debate.

These 137 TSUSA numbers were submitted to a Commerce Department data base at the National Institute of Health computer center and monthly data were requested. These data were forwarded to the author in the form of a computer tape for use on a mainframe computer. Gathering these data by hand from hard-copy sources was deemed infeasible not only because of the massive size of the data base but also because the Commerce Department publication in which monthly TSUSA data are reported by trading partner (IM146) is not widely disseminated. Neither U.S. Government Depositories, such as the library at the University of North Carolina, nor regional offices of the Commerce Department, such as the one in Greensboro, North Carolina that assisted the present author in the electronic gathering of data, receive this publication.

This initial sample of 137 products was examined in greater detail upon the receipt of the data tape. This examination revealed severe problems with heterogeneity in some products from certain countries. For example, in four cylinder autos imported from Germany the prices fluctuated wildly from month to month. This might be explained by the fact that in some months the majority of these autos were manufactured by Volkswagen and in other months the majority were manufactured by Mercedes or BMW. This difference in the composition of imports for this particular TSUSA number would certainly result in this wild fluctuation of unit values. However, a product demonstrating this sort of unit value behavior must be eliminated from the sample because a factor other than exchange rates (or even costs) is driving these changes.

This sort of heterogeneous unit value behavior resulted in the elimination of some TSUSA categories entirely while in oher instances only certain countries were eliminated. In the case of four cylinder autos the elimination of German autos did not necessitate the removal of Japanese or Korean autos from the sample. The end result was that an additional 25 product categories were excluded from the final sample. This left 112 seven-digit TSUSA product categories to be analyzed for pass-through behavior with 30 being consumer non-durables, 31 consumer durables, 34 intermediate goods, and 17 capital goods (see Table 4.3 for a synopsis of the major steps leading to this final sample of 112 TSUSA product categories.)

Table 4.3
The Path Leading to the 112 Product Categories
Included in the Final Sample

Original # of 7-digit TSUSA categories	>16,000
# left after $75 million rule applied	874
# left after additional rules applied	98
# included by selectively completing certain pricing series	+38
# included by use of schedules 1 & 2	+4
# included by allowing terms such as "etc."	+9
# excluded by initial examination for heterogeneity	-12
Net # submitted for electronic data collection	137
# excluded after additional examination for heterogeneity	-25
Net # of product categories included in final sample	112

Many of the products deleted due to excessive heterogeneity were capital goods. This does not come as a shock since many such high-value products are customized to individual customer needs and, as a result, are very different from each other. The shortage of products that fit into the capital goods product type also led to the inclusion of several product categories that could easily have been classified as intermediate goods or consumer durables. For a complete breakdown of the 112 products included in the final sample by product-type, see Appendix C. This appendix also includes the dollar value of imports for each product category in 1988.

DATA ON BI-LATERAL EXCHANGE RATES

As mentioned earlier, the vast majority of previous pass-through research has examined highly aggregated data. This has led researchers to utilize various types of composites, or baskets, of exchange rates of major trading countries as the exchange rate variable in their pass-through models. Since all exchange rates are bi-lateral (or country-specific) by their very nature and one of the objectives of this research is to examine import pricing behavior at more micro levels than previous studies, the decision was made to examine U.S. import prices on a bi-lateral basis. This necessitates the use of bi-lateral exchange rates.

The monthly exchange rate data for eighteen of the twenty countries included in the sample will be obtained from the International Monetary Fund (IMF) publication, *International Financial Statistics*. Exchange rates for Taiwan and Hong Kong are not reported by the IMF, so these rates will be gathered from the *World Currency Handbook*. The use of two different sources of exchange rate data could introduce a bias into this variable but is unavoidable if Taiwan and Hong Kong are to be included.

COUNTRIES INCLUDED IN THE SAMPLE

A choice of countries to be included in the project had to be made. The basic criterion utilized was that a country must be one of the twenty largest importers into the U.S. across all non-oil imports. This decision rule was based on total imports for the year 1988.

The country-selection decision rule was violated in two situations. The lack of convertibility of the currency of the Peoples' Republic of China during the time period of the sample led to the elimination of the PRC from the sample.

The other exception to the country-selection decision rule was Argentina. The fact that two other Latin American countries (Brazil and

Mexico) which experienced hyper-inflationary situations during the time period of the sample were already included led to the decision to eliminate Argentina. The effect of the hyper-inflation on the currencies of these Latin American countries was of such a tremendous magnitude that any pass-through results could prove to be questionable. Argentina was eliminated because the magnitude of its imports to the U.S. was the smallest of the three.

The twenty countries finally included in the sample are listed in Table 4.4. While some of these countries managed their currencies in a somewhat rigid fashion during the time frame of the sample, there was some degree of float allowed in the bulk of the time period for almost all countries. For detailed information on these countries' currency regimes during the time periods of this study, the reader can refer to the IMF publication, *International Financial Statistics*.

Table 4.4
Countries Included in the Sample

Belgium	Japan	Spain
Brazil	Korea, South	Sweden
Canada	Malaysia	Switzerland
France	Mexico	Taiwan
Germany, West	Netherlands	Thailand
Hong Kong	Philippines	United Kingdom
Italy	Singapore	

SCOPE OF FINAL SAMPLE

After following the procedure for product category sample selection there were 112 seven-digit TSUSA product categories included in the sample. These 112 product categories accounted for 14.36 percent of total U.S. imports in 1988 (see Table 4.5) even though they comprised less than one percent of the over 16,000 seven-digit TSUSA categories.

Table 4.5
Highlights of 1988 U.S. Import Data
and of the Final Sample Data

Total Imports	$437,140,185,000.00
Total Value of 7-digit TSUSA #'s Exceeding $75 million in Imports	$345,765,280,000.00
Total Value of 7-digit TSUSA #'s Included in the Final Sample	$ 62,772,028,000.00
Percentage of Total Imports Contained in the Categories Included in the Sample	14.36%

When measuring pass-through for these 112 product categories only those countries that accounted for at least 10 percent of import volume (by value or quantity) for that product were considered. For example, if for a particular product there were three "major" importers, there would be three measurements of pass-through. A country must have been one of the twenty previously selected for inclusion in the sample for its imports to be examined. This process led to a final sample of 258 product/country combinations (e.g., 13-inch color TV's from Malaysia). The "10 percent of imports" decision rule resulted in 26 of the 7-digit categories being represented by only one importing country. The other 86 categories were represented by from two to six importing countries with the average number of importing countries per product being 2.7 (see Table 4.6 for a synopsis of some of these sample characteristics). The 258 measurements of product-specific pass-through behavior are the largest number of pass-through measurements ever made in one study. Appendix B contains a complete listing of the 112 TSUSA categories included in the final sample and the countries that met the ten percent criterion for each.

Table 4.6
Some Characteristics of the Final Sample

# of 7-digit TSUSA categories included	112
# of Product/Country combinations	258
Mean # of competitors (countries) per product category	2.3
# of product categories represented by only one country	26
# of product categories represented by multiple countries	86
Mean # of competitors (countries) per category for those categories represented by multiple countries	2.7
Maximum # of competitors (countries) representing a single product category	6

Tables 4.7 through 4.11 summarize some additional aspects of the final sample. Both individual 7-digit TSUSA product categories and product types are reviewed. It is interesting to note that auto imports alone account for almost 52 percent of the total value of the final sample.

Table 4.7

Fifteen Product Categories from Sample with Greatest Dollar
Volume of Imports in 1988 in Millions of Dollars

Product	$ Volume	% Increase 1979-88	# Countries
New 4-cyl. autos other than sta. wagons & vans	20974	120	3
Autos over 4 but not over 6 cyl.	9193	345	3
VCR's	2506	644	3
Autos over 6 cyl.	2419	402	1
Leather footwear, women, cement sole, over $2.50	1746	237	3
Leather athletic ftwr., male, nspf	1323	669	2
Electrostatic copy machine	1175	355	1
Piston-type auto, truck & bus eng., excluding diesel	1092	285	3
Radial auto tires	1091	106	6
Uranium Fluorides	851	81	1
Beer	820	167	4
Other truck and bus tires, radial	600	.4	3
Microwave ovens	577	254	3
Leather athletic footwear, women & misses, over $2.50	562	1838	2
13 inch color TV's	526	748	5

Table 4.8
Fifteen Product Categories from Sample with Largest
Percentage Increases in Total Value of Imports: 1979-1988

Product	% Increase U.S. Imports
Air cond. & refrig. compres., 1/4 hp or less	62700
Bicycles over 25 in., over $16.66, not elsewhere specified	8731
Writing Paper	2124
Leather athletic footwear, women & misses, over $2.50	1838
Coffee makers	1536
Battery charging generators and alternators	1203
Stuffed animals over a specific value	1202
Air cond. & refrig. compres., over 1/4 hp, not over 1 hp	1045
Sodium Hydroxide	834
13 inch color TV's	748
Rubber or plastic bags, etc.	698
Leather athletic footwear, male, not specifically provided for	669
Ball-point pens and pencils	663
VCR's	644
Perfume, cologne, etc.	634

Table 4.9
Breakdown of Sample by Product Type
(Value in Millions of U.S. Dollars)

Product Type	#	Total Value	% Imports	% of Sample
Cons. Dur.*	31	$40,231	9.20	64.1
Cons. ND	30	$10,098	2.31	16.1
Inter. Gd.	34	$ 8,308	1.90	13.2
Cap. Gd.	17	$ 4,135	0.95	6.6
Total	112	$62,772	14.36	100.0

*Note: $32,586 million of total imports are in three 7-digit TSUSA
numbers for automobiles. 4, 6, and 8-cylinder autos account
for 51.9% of the total sample by dollar volume.

Table 4.10
Breakdown of Sample by Country

Country	# of Products	Country	# of Products
Japan	57	United Kingdom	10
Taiwan	40	Italy	8
S. Korea	33	Singapore	7
Canada	20	France	7
Germany	19	Spain	5
Mexico	18	Malaysia	4
Brazil	12	Netherlands	3
Hong Kong	11	Sweden	3
Philippines	1		

Table 4.11
Breakdown of Sample by Region

Region	# of Products	# Countries in Region
Pacific Rim	153	7
Western Europe	55	7
Canada and Mexico*	38	2
Latin America	12	1

V

Research Method:
Pass-Through Estimation

In this chapter the model to be utilized in the measurement of pass-through for the 258 product/country combinations will be fully explained. This explanation will include discussions of: (1) the use of a log-log model for the measurement of pass-through, (2) the use of first differencing on the variables, (3) the type of lag structure to be utilized in the measurement process, (4) the number of lags of the exchange rate variable that will be used, (5) the assumptions that are being made when using the measurement model, (6) what the actual measurement of pass-through will consist of, and (7) the exclusion of explanatory variables other than the exchange rate variable and its lags from the pass-through measurement model.

THE BASIC MODEL

The basic relationship between import prices and exchange rates implied by the law of one price can be summarized as follows:

Foreign Price = Home Price * Exchange Rate.

This can be manipulated to show that the following relationships exist:

$$P_F/P_H = e$$

Where P_F = the price of a domestically produced product being sold in a foreign market expressed in the foreign currency,

P_H = the domestic price of a domestically produced product expressed in the home currency, and

e = the rate of exchange between the foreign and home currencies.

A different manipulation yields the following relationship:

$$P_H = P_F/e.$$

This basic relationship, and its variations created by algebraic manipulation, is the basis for the law of one price. This relationship implies complete and immediate pass-through if one assumes that each good in an economy is treated independently so that price changes by an exporter to the U.S. are not in response to a change in the general price level in the U.S. market but in response to an independently generated change in the exchange rate. Such a relationship would logically hold if none of the conditions outlined in Chapter 2 that would result in incomplete pass-through existed and if: (1) arbitrage activities were possible (i.e., price discrimination across markets is not possible), (2) the response of import prices to exchange rate changes was symmetrical (i.e., prices go both up and down in a proportional relationship to exchange rate changes), (3) the response of prices to exchange rate changes was immediate.

        If an accomodation is made to allow for the response of import prices to exchange rate fluctuations to occur over time, rather than immediately, the following relationship would exist:

$$IP_t = f(FP_t, FX_{t.t-n})$$

Where IP_t = contemporaneous import price in U.S. dollars

        FP_t = contemporaneous price in foreign currency of imported product in the foreign market where it is produced and exported from.

        $FX_{t.n}$ = contemporaneous and lagged values of the exchange rate (U.S. dollar/foreign currency).

This model simply asserts that the import price of a product at time *t* is a function of that product's domestic price in the exporting country (expressed in the currency of the exporting country) and the contemporaneous and some number of lagged values of the exchange rate between the currencies of the importing and exporting countries.

        The inclusion of lagged values of the exchange rate as explanators of contemporaneous import prices allows this process of adjustment to a new equilibrium necessitated by fluctuations in exchange rates to occur over time rather than instantaneously. This adjustment process could be explained by appealing to a theoretical explanation such as adaptive expectations (i.e., a person's expectation of the future is based on a process wherein information from the present and past time periods are weighted to form an opinion of what to expect in the future). In a related vein, one might assume that it takes time to perceive what the new economic environment will be and to implement decisions once they are made. One might also hypothesize that information and transactions costs would mitigate against hasty decisions in response to changes in one's environment. The idea could even be advanced that a firm would hesitate to pass along the full force of a major exchange rate fluctuation immediately due to the possibility of shocking consumers or because market conditions simply would not allow such an action. Making such a market-oriented price adjustment over time would allow for a gradual process of acceptance of changing prices to occur.

Lags in the reaction of certain import prices to exchange rate changes might also result from the existence of contracted prices that are not subject to change for some specified period of time. Such lags could also be more apparent than real. The lags could be caused by reporting delays in the bureaucratic system through which such data are handled or by the necessity for long periods of product transport in international trade. Whatever the explanation, the inclusion of a temporal element in the relationship between changes in exchange rates and changes in import prices allows for the possibility of some sort of an adjustment process occuring rather than requiring that all adjustment occur instantly.

EXPRESSION OF THE RELATIONSHIP IN MULTIPLICATIVE FORM

One method for allowing the impact of exchange rate changes on import price changes to be felt over time is by expressing the relationship between these variables in multiplicative form. This allows for the possibility that the contemporaneous value or certain lagged values of the exchange rate variable might have a greater effect on a product's import price than certain other of the lags of this variable. In multiplicative form the model would appear as follows:

$$IP_t = FP_t * FX_t^{b1} * FX_{t-1}^{b2} * ... * FX_{t-n}^{bn+1}.$$

Where IP_t = the U.S. import price of the product at time t expressed
in U.S. dollars per unit,

FP_t = the price of the product at time t in the foreign market
of production and exportation expressed in the domestic
currency (e.g., yen per unit), and

$FX_{t..t-n}$ = the contemporaneous (time t) and lagged exchange rates
expressed as U.S. dollars per unit of the foreign
currency (e.g., \$2/pound or \$.005/yen).

The exponents (b's) of the contemporaneous and lagged values
of the exchange rate are interpreted as the elasticities of import price
with respect to the various lags of the exchange rate. If the elasticity of
the contemporaneous value of the exchange rate (b_1) equals one and the
elasticities of all its lags $(b_2..b_n)$ are zero, the implication is that all
changes in exchange rates are immediately reflected in changes in the
import price. If the import price adjustment to changes in exchange
rates occurs over time, the value of b_1 and several of the elasticities of
the lagged exchange rate values would be between zero and one. If
pass-through were 100 percent, the sum of the elasticities would be one.

THE MODEL TO BE ESTIMATED

Several transformations must be made to the above model in
preparation for the introduction of the actual regression model to be
used in the present study for the measurement of pass-through. These
transformations and the nature of the lag structure for the exchange rate
variable are discussed below.

Log-Log Transformation of the Model

To improve the interpretability of regression-based estimation
of the above multiplicative model a transformation to natural logarithms
will be made. Both the dependent variable and the independent variables
will be transformed into the natural logarithm form. The resulting model

is easily interpretable since the coefficients of the contemporaneous and lagged values of the exchange rate variable become elasticities and these elasticities are constant over all values of the import price variable and for any given lag of the exchange rate variable.

First-Differencing of Variables

Another feature of the pass-through measurement model will be the expression of the natural logarithms of import prices and exchange rates as changes, or first-differences. The expression of these variables as first-differences happens to serve the useful functions of: (1) detrending the data, with the incumbent imposition of a more stationary covariance structure on the error term, thus ameliorating potential problems with excessive serial correlation in the untransformed variable, and (2) reducing the likelihood of regression coefficients being statistically significant due only to random processes occuring in the untransformed data, or the problem of "spurious" regression.

The use of differencing for nothing more than the above reasons has come under criticism in recent years. Williams (1978) is highly critical of the use of first differences as a solution for problems with stationarity. He claims that a data set should be empirically tested so that problems of non-stationarity can be verified prior to the use of first-differencing. Williams then explains that such empirical testing of a data set is not feasible with a "finite" data set and that an a priori assumption of problems with non-stationarity is not justified.

Williams also claims that most economic relationships are crude approximations to reality and to insist on proper estimation techniques is over-zealous. He concludes by commenting that, "A pragmatic approach would be to estimate such models using least-squares procedures [using levels instead of resorting to differencing] without worrying too much about the properties of the error structure."

While Williams' contentions are debatable, the use of differencing in this study is appropriate for reasons not related to problems of non-stationarity of the error term or "spurious" regression. It is intuitively appealing that importers are responding to changes in exchange rates rather than levels of these rates as they adjust prices. If this is the case, then differencing is justified on the grounds that this is the model that reflects reality.

Lag Structure of the Exchange Rate Variable

As can be seen from an examination of Table 2.2, there have been two basic types of constrained distributed lag structures utilized in the regression models that measured pass-through in previous empirical research utilizing disaggregated data (the term distributed lag means that the relative beta weights (coefficients) of the lagged variable's values are apportioned, or distributed, among the lags so that some lags are more important than others in determining the impact of the explanatory variable(s) on the dependent variable). One type is the ordinary least squares (OLS) approach in which the only constraint imposed on the distributed lag structure is to limit the number of lags of the exchange rate variable to some finite number. All six of the time series studies summarized in Table 2.2 reported the use of such a model.

In its simplest form, this general model postulates that some regressor (in the present case the exchange rate variable) has a long-lasting effect on the dependent variable (the import price variable).[1] In a completely unconstrained distributed lag model, the impact of lagged values of the exchange rate variable would be infinite. The constraint on the number of lags included in the model is necessary in almost any distributed lag model as the number of observations available in time series is usually limited. The choice as to the appropriate number of lags to include is a difficult one and must ultimately be made by the individual researcher based on his thoughts and experiences.

The second type of constrained distributed lag structure that has been utilized in several of these more micro-level empirical studies is that of a second-degree polynomial (PDL). Three of the six time series studies summarized in Table 2.2 reported results of such a model.

The PDL technique for dealing with distributed lag models involves the imposition of a priori expectations on the shape of the distributed lag coefficients. The PDL assumes that the lag coefficients are shaped in the form of a polynomial. Several authors have expressed concerns about the severity of the constraints that a polynomial structure imposes on the coefficients of the lagged variable and the difficulty inherent in determining whether a second-degree or higher degree polynomial lag structure is appropriate.[2] Authors such as Kmenta (1986) have also lamented the arbitrariness of the approach to deciding what types of constraints (in addition to the constraints imposed on the individual regression coefficients) will be imposed on PDL's. For example, some researchers impose so-called "end-point" restrictions which constrain the values of the coefficients of the lagged variable at times *t* - *1* and *t* + *number of lags included* + *1* to be equal to zero. While the imposition of such additional constraints tends to further dampen erratic behavior of the coefficients (e.g., alternating positive and negative coefficients), it also limits the degree to which the data are allowed to "speak for themselves."

The advisability of utilizing a PDL or some other distributed lag structure that imposes numerous constraints on the behavior of the coefficients of the lagged values of the explantory variable(s) rather than a general distributed lag structure constrained only by the number of lags included is discussed by Cassidy (1981). He observes that, "Many researchers do not wish to estimate this type of equation [distributed lag] directly [through the use of a general distributed lag model] and instead use some indirect procedures [e.g., PDL]. They avoid direct estimation because (1) there may not be enough observations relative to the number of parameters that need to be estimated, i.e., the degrees of freedom problem; or (2) the values of X [in this study the exchange rate variable] and its lagged values may be collinear, which implies that the individual effect of any one of them, . . . , on the dependent variable [in this study the import price variable] could not be reliably estimated, i.e., the problem of multicollinearity."

Cassidy continues to say that, "Econometricians should reconsider their reluctance to estimate this equation directly. One should use one's priors to reduce the number of lagged terms as much as possible (that is, reduce the length of the lag, m), so that both problems are at least ameliorated. The fewer the number of regressors, the fewer the number of parameters to estimate and the fewer the variables that are collinear. In addition, the types of indirect estimation techniques usually employed impose a different set of priors, the validity of which may be questioned."

A concern for the implications of the imposition of questionable assumptions on the distributed lag structure led the present author to choose to estimate a regression-based model for measuring pass-through in the most general form possible. An initial decision was made to avoid the use of the indirect estimation techniques such as the PDL structure in favor of the use of OLS regression with unconstrained coefficients on the explanatory variables. The only constraint imposed was the limitation of the number of lagged values of the exchange rate variable to be included in the estimation model. The importance of the decision to avoid the use of a PDL structure is diminished by the fact that both Feenstra (1989) and Hooper and Mann (1989) found non-significant differences between the pass-through measurements yielded by a distributed lag structure whose coefficients were constrained to the form of a second-degree polynomial and the simpler, general distributed lag structure constrained only by a limit on the number of lagged values of the exchange rate variable.

Number of Lags to be Included

Goldstein and Khan (1984) and Kenen and Pack (1980) cite empirical studies of pass-through conducted using sample time frames during the period of flexible exchange rates which indicate that, to whatever extent pass-through occurs, the process is complete within six to nine months. Goldstein and Khan state, ". . . time lags in the import price pass-through are short; typically the effect is complete in six months . . . " They do go on to caution that such a short adjustment period may not be the case for a large country such as the United States.

As mentioned in the literature review, the 1983 study by the U.S. International Trade Commission found that for a limited number of 4-digit SITC products a lag of one or two quarters was adequate for capturing the pass-through effect. Feenstra (1989) included four quarterly lags in his pass-through measurement model but found that the process was basically complete within three quarters. Hooper and Mann (1989) found the lag to take place over five to seven quarters. However, their inclusion of non-significant coefficients of lagged values of the exchange rate variable in their calculation of pass-through rates is cause for concern and leads one to question their results. This is especially true since in most cases all lags of the exchange rate variable past four quarters failed to demonstrate statistical significance.

With previous theoretical and empirical studies in mind, the decision was made to include twelve lagged values of the monthly exchange rate variable along with the contemporaneous exchange rate as explanatory variables in the pass-through measurement model. The decision to include twelve lags, rather than six or nine, of the exchange rate variable was made in an effort to ensure that incomplete pass-through is fully demonstrated while avoiding the difficulties, such as spurious correlation or excessive multicollinearity, involved with interpretation of regression coefficients when an excessive number of lags are included.

The Pass-Through Measurement Model

After making the transformation to natural logarithms, expressing the variables in the form of first differences, and including the twelve lagged values of the exchange rate variable, the actual regression model to be estimated for the purpose of measuring pass-through is as follows:

$$\Delta lnIP_t = b_0 + b_1 \Delta lnFX_t + b_2 \Delta lnFX_{t-1} + \ldots + b_{13} \Delta lnFX_{t-12} + e_t$$

Where $\Delta lnIP_t$ = change in the natural logarithm of the Import Price from previous month

$\Delta lnFX_t$ = change in the natural logarithm of the exchange rate from previous month

b_0 = intercept term

$b_{1..13}$ = regression coefficients for the contemporaneous and 12 monthly lags of the change in the natural logarithm of the exchange rate

e_t = error term

Pass-Through = $\sum b_1..b_{13}$ and is not constrained to the range of zero to one or to be positive.

In the above formulation the intercept term (b_0) is effectively made a surrogate for the foreign price of the imported product expressed in the domestic currency of the importing country (FP_t in the untransformed multiplicative versions of the model). This surrogacy occurs due to the exclusion of an actual foreign price. It should be noted that all exchange rates are expressed as U.S. dollars per unit of foreign currency. This allows the regression coefficients to be positive when import prices (expressed in U.S. dollars) and exchange rates are moving in the same direction as would be expected.

It is presumed that the basic assumptions of classical OLS multiple regression will be met by the proposed model. Specifically, it is assumed that: (1) the error term is normally distributed, (2) the expected value of the error term is zero, (3) the variance of the error term is constant for all observations (no heteroskedasticity), (4) the disturbance occurring at one point of observation is not correlated with any other disturbance (no serial correlation), and (5) no exact linear relation exists between any of the explanatory variables (no multicollinearity).

The two basic assumptions that are most likely to be violated and to cause serious problems with interpretation of the regression coefficients in an analysis of an economic time series are those of no serial correlation and no multicollinearity. The appropriateness of these assumptions will be tested through the use of commonly accepted methods for the detection of excessive serial correlation (Durbin-Watson test) and excessive multicollinearity (variance inflation factor) in the process of estimating the regression model (these methods of detection are discussed in the presentation of results).

If the assumption of no serial correlation is found to be violated, remedial action will be taken in the form of estimating a transformed regression equation that is commonly referred to as the Prais-Winsten two-step method. This transformation will be detailed below in the event that its use is necessary. If excessive multicollinearity is detected the only viable recourse is to report the problem and elaborate on the potential problems it causes in interpretation of the regression results.

OTHER ASSUMPTIONS OF THE MODEL

The study will emphasize the effects that exchange rate changes have on import prices, rather than any potential effects that import prices might have on exchange rates. This implies the use of a non-recursive model.

The choice of a non-recursive model is based on two considerations.[3] First, if exchange rates are primarily determined in asset markets (Kenen and Pack (1980) contend that theories advocating this basic premise are dominant amongst economists today), one would not anticipate a strong causal linkage running from import price changes to exchange rate changes. Under such a view of exchange rate determination short term expectations about rates of return on various assets (including foreign exchange) would dominate the value placed on any particular currency. As a result, import price changes could influence exchange rate changes only when such price changes lead to expectations of exchange rate changes. It would also be necessary for these expectations of exchange rate changes based on trade or import price changes to overwhelm all other information on which these markets base their expectations about rates of return. This scenario seems unlikely.

The second reason for the use of a non-recursive relationship between import prices and exchange rates is empirically based. Kenen and Pack (1980) analyzed the relationship between these two variables running in both directions. They found a statistically significant relationship running from exchange rates to prices but no such relationship running from prices to exchange rates. Goldstein (1979) also points out that the bulk of research on PPP tends to support the PPP idea in the long-run but not in the short-run. This means that differences between national inflation rates do not produce offsetting changes in exchange rates in a short-term framework such as the one adopted in the present study. These considerations seem to justify the assumption of a non-recursive relationship.

The exploratory nature of the study also leads to the choice of a partial equilibrium model in which it is assumed that exchange rates are an exogenous variable. The development of a more general and complete empirical model of import price changes that entails a system of equations examining the factors that influence movements in exchange rates will be left to future research. This simplifying assumption is reasonable in exploratory research and has been made in all previous pass-through research. The focus of the present research is on the measurement of pass-through and does not necessitate a more complex model.

There is also an implicit assumption in this research that markets for foreign exchange are efficient. Actual exchange rates, as opposed to exchange rate expectations, are utilized in the pass-through measurement model. This implies that importers feel that the present exchange rate is the best predictor of future exchange rates. There are many alternatives for arriving at a value of the expected exchange rate and the use of one of these might be appropriate as this research stream becomes more refined.

An assumption that change will be continual is also built into the pass-through equation. Since both exchange rates and import prices are being analyzed as changes, rather than levels, there is an implication that changes in exchange rates and import prices will continue into the future. This seems justified as long as free or quasi-free foreign exchange markets exist for major trading nations so that floating rates will continue to be predominant.

EXCLUSION OF OTHER POSSIBLE EXPLANATORY VARIABLES

The exploratory nature of the present research led to the decision to exclude any explanatory variables other than the exchange rate variable and its lags. This has the potential for causing problems as the omission of relevant variables can lead to biased coefficients for the exchange rate variable and its lags in the pass-through measurement model. This problem is not uncommon in empirical research.

The variable whose exclusion from the measurement model might cause the greatest concern in an attempt to explain changes in price is the imported product's cost of production. Two considerations should be mentioned in regards to this variable: (1) many major U.S. imports are in industries that are mature in most of the industrialized world and in which changes in production costs are minimal and infrequent, and (2) the likelihood of major changes occurring in an importer's production costs (expressed in the domestic currency of the importer) during the twelve month period of adjustment built into the measurement model is not high (even though the time frame of the sample is ten years, the adjustment of import prices to changes in exchange rates is assumed to take place over a twelve month period, which means that the changes in variables such as cost would not be impacting the measurement model outside of this twelve month time period). These factors should greatly alleviate the concerns regarding the omission of production costs from the model as it may not actually be a relevant variable under these circumstances.

There is also a problem with a lack of knowledge as to where the inputs of a product originated. For example, the major components of a television imported from Japan might come from several countries.

This international sourcing introduces uncertainty into attempts to include aspects of production costs such as labor. This means that an attempt to include estimates of production costs (or some proxy thereof such as labor costs) could actually worsen rather than solve problems with misspecification.

Other explanatory variables could be advanced in a model measuring pass-through. Previous studies have seen the inclusion of variables such as the prices of domestic substitutes for an imported product and a surrogate for the structure of the industry in which a product is produced. However, the inclusion of such variables through the use of a possibly ill-defined proxy for them in an exploratory study of this type does not seem advisable. The basic relationship between import prices and exchange rates should first be examined. A more complete model will be left to future research.

NOTES

1. Much of the discussion of distributed lag models is owing to the work of Henry J. Cassidy in *Using Econometrics: A Beginner's Guide*, Reston Publishing Co., Inc., Reston, VA., 1981.

2. See Kmenta, Jan, *Elements of Econometrics*, 2nd edition, 1986, Macmillan, New York and Cassidy, Henry J., *Using Econometrics: A Beginner's Guide*, Reston Publishing Co., Inc., Reston, VA., 1981, for a more thorough discussion of some of the problems inherent in the use of polynomial lag structures.

3. This part of the discussion is owing to Kenen, Peter B. and C. Pack, "Exchange Rates and Domestic Prices: A Survey of the Evidence," research memorandum, International Finance Section, Princeton University, Princeton, 1980.

VI

Research Method:
Research Design

This chapter will give a breakdown of the different regression runs that will be made in the pass-through measurement model. These different runs are necessary in order to test whether there is a difference in pass-through behavior for periods of exchange rate depreciation and appreciation, that is whether or not the response of import prices to exchange rate changes is symmetrical.

SUB-PERIODS OF APPRECIATION
AND DEPRECIATION

In addition to examining the entire time frame of the sample, certain sub-periods were examined that corresponded to the major changes in direction of the exchange rates of the countries included in the sample. This part of the analysis was conducted in an effort to determine whether the reaction of import prices to exchange rate changes was symmetrical, that is whether the response to an appreciation was the same as the response to a depreciation and vice versa.

Table 6.1 gives a breakdown of the periods of appreciation, depreciation, and basic stability for the currencies of those countries that were used in the study *vis-a-vis* the U.S. dollar. A period of appreciation means that the value of the foreign currency (e.g., British pound) was appreciating in U.S. dollar terms. As mentioned previously, all exchange rates are expressed as U.S. dollars per unit of foreign currency so that the regression coefficients of the exchange rate variable and its lags will be positive when import prices and exchange rates are moving in the same direction.

Table 6.1

Sub-Periods of Major Movements in
Foreign Exchange Rates: 1979 - 1988

Country	Appreciation(s)	Depreciation(s)	Stable
W. Europe*		1/79-3/85	
	3/85-12/88		
Japan		1/79-10/82	
			10/82-9/85
	9/85-12/88		
Canada		1/79-1/86	
	1/86-12/88		
U.K.	1/79-1/81		
		1/81-3/85	
	3/85-12/88		
S. Korea		1/80-9/85	
	9/85-12/88		
Taiwan		1/79-9/83	
	9/83-12/88		
Hong Kong		1/79-9/83	
			9/83-12/88
Singapore	1/79-12/81		
		12/81-2/85	
	2/85-12/88		
Malaysia	1/79-9/80		
		9/80-12/88	

Note: Brazil, Mexico, and the Philippines experienced steady depreciations of their currencies over the entire period of the sample, so no sub-periods existed.
*Includes Belgium, France, Germany, Italy, Netherlands, Spain, Sweden, and Switzerland.

OTHER MEASURES OF PASS-THROUGH

In addition to the general distributed lag pass-through measurement model and its transformed version utilized to correct for excessive serial correlation that were developed in Chapter 5, two supplementary measures of pass-through will be computed. A second regression-based measurement model in which the regression coefficients of the distributed lag of the exchange rate variable are constrained to follow the shape of a second-degree polynomial will be analyzed. This second-degree polynomially distributed lag (PDL) model will also be analyzed for both the entire time frame of the sample and for sub-periods of currency appreciation and depreciation. This measurement model is detailed in Chapter 7.

Finally, a non-regression-based pass-through measurement will be computed. The end-point method discussed in Chapter 2 will be used for this purpose. It will also be discussed further in Chapter 7.

VII

Data Analysis and Results

This chapter details the process of analyzing the data. Preliminary analyses such as a graphical examination of import price and exchange rate variables are discussed. The results of the pass-through measurement models are presented and some of the limitations of the measurement process are discussed.

PRELIMINARY ANALYSIS TOOLS

The first analysis tool utilized was a graphical analysis of the two principal variables, import prices and exchange rates. Plots were made of the import prices (unit values) of all 258 product/country combinations and of exchange rates for all 20 countries for the time span of the sample (in a few cases the series were plotted only for selected sub-periods because the series did not cover the entire time span or the unit values were so erratic that it was obvious the changes in price were driven by changes in the composition of imports). Graphs of the 20 exchange rate series were overlaid on the price graph for the appropriate product/country combinations for comparison purposes.

The behaviors of import prices and exchange rates were compared for both the overall time period of the sample and all sub-periods of exchange rate appreciation/depreciation. This visual inspection resulted in choosing 36 combinations in which there appeared to be a fairly close relationship between the movements in import prices and exchange rates. In many cases the movements of the two variables were in opposite directions. Figures 7.1 and 7.2 are examples of this type of graphical presentation of the data.[1]

Another preliminary analysis involved a univariate analysis of the exchange rate time series of all 20 countries included in the sample. This analysis included an indication of the amount of variation in each exchange rate time series and provided other descriptive statistics as

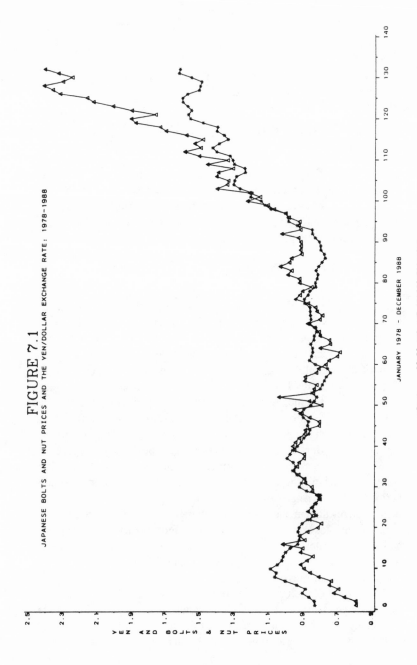

FIGURE 7.1

JAPANESE BOLTS AND NUT PRICES AND THE YEN/DOLLAR EXCHANGE RATE: 1978-1988

JANUARY 1978 - DECEMBER 1988

YEN=•   BOLTS AND NUT PRICES=TRIANGLE

FIGURE 7.2

MEXICAN ELECTRIC MOTOR PRICES AND THE PESO/DOLLAR EXCHANGE RATE: 1983-1988

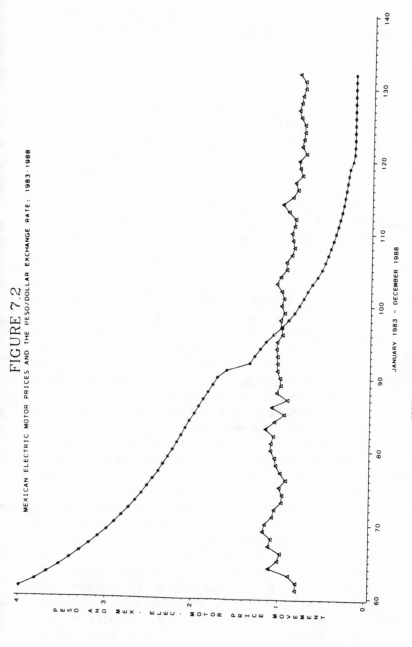

JANUARY 1983 – DECEMBER 1988

PESO=*   MEXICAN ELECTRIC MOTOR PRICES=TRIANGLE

well. Table 7.1 summarizes these analyses for the Canadian Dollar, Taiwanese Newdollar, Japanese Yen, and South Korean Won.

Table 7.1

Results of Univariate Analysis of Selected
Standarized Exchange Rate Time Series

Currency	Standard Deviation	Minimum	Maximum
Canadian Dollar	0.0722575	1.00000	1.27745
Taiwanese Newdollar	0.1171540	0.87841	1.35377
Japanese Yen	0.2501120	0.73718	1.62408
South Korean Won	0.2869900	0.99808	1.83994

The limited amount of variation in some of the exchange rate time series (e.g., the Canadian Dollar and the Taiwanese Newdollar) is potentially troublesome because this condition could cause the regression coefficients of the contemporary and lagged values of the explanatory variable (change in the natural logarithm of the exchange rate) in the pass-through measurement model to have high levels of variation. High values of these coefficient standard errors would make interpretation of these coefficients difficult. This will be discussed further below as multicollinearity is explored.

A final preliminary analysis involved the computation of Pearson product-moment correlations. These correlations were calculated for changes in the natural logarithms of import prices and the changes in the natural logarithms of the contemporaneous exchange rate and six lags thereof. This measure of association served as a preliminary indication of whether import prices move in fairly close relation to exchange rates. Six lags of the exchange rate variable were included because it was felt that this would provide ample time for some association to be demonstrated even if the adjustment process takes longer than this to be completed. Of the 258 product/country combinations there were only 88 that demonstrated at least one statistically significant positive correlation (at the .05 level) between the import price variable and any of the lags of the exchange rate variable.

Only 49 of these had significant positive correlations for either the overall time frame or a sub-period of sixty-five or more months. This supplemented the graphical indications that the relationship between changes in import prices and changes in exchange rates might not be especially strong.

REGRESSION-BASED PASS-THROUGH MEASRUEMENT MODEL

Pass-through was initially measured for all product/country combinations by utilizing the regression model developed in Chapter 5. In this model the distributed lag structure was constrained only by the number of lags of the exchange rate variable to be included as explanatory variables. As detailed in Chapter 5, the measurement model is as follows:

$$\Delta \ln IP_t = b_0 + b_1 \Delta \ln FX_t + b_2 \Delta \ln FX_{t-1} + ... + b_{13} \Delta \ln FX_{t-12} + e_t$$

Where $\Delta \ln IP_t$ = change in the natural logarithm of the Import Price from previous month

$\Delta \ln FX_t$ = change in the log of the exchange rate

b_0 = intercept term

$b_{1..13}$ = coefficients for the contemporaneous and 12 monthly lags of the exchange rate variable

e_t = error term

Pass-Through = $\sum b_1 .. b_{13}$

The assumptions informing the model were discussed in Chapter 5.

This general model was examined for the price series of all 258 product/country combinations and the entire span of the series for which prices were available. The pricing series were also examined utilizing this measurement model for the sub-periods of currency appreciation and depreciation that were indicated in Table 6.1.

Testing and Correcting for Serial Correlation

A potentially serious statistical problem could develop with excessive serial correlation of the error terms. The degree of serial correlation was tested through the use of the Durbin-Watson statistic.

While the Durbin-Watson test is designed to detect problems with excessive first-order serial correlation, Kmenta (1986) indicates that it is robust to the detection of higher order serial correlation. Since the present study utilizes monthly data it seems possible that the disturbances could be characterized by a twelfth-order rather than a first-order autoregressive process. It was decided that the robust nature of the statistic should make it a useful test for excessive serial correlation in this exploratory study.

For those product/country combinations that exhibited high levels of serial correlation of the error terms as determined by the Durbin-Watson statistic, a transformation commonly referred to as the "Prais-Winsten transformation" was utilized. After the general model was transformed it was re-estimated.[2] This transformation was developed by econometricians in response to concerns raised over the fact that the well-known "Cochrane-Orcutt" transformation for handling excessive serial correlation led to the loss of one observation from the time series being analyzed. The Prais-Winsten transformation seems to be more commonly used in econometrics today than the Cochrane-Orcutt method. This transformation is accomplished by multiplying all terms in the regression equation by the term $\sqrt{1-\rho^2}$ prior to re-estimation of the regression equation. ρ (rho) is the coefficient of correlation and must be calculated for use in the transformation.

Testing for Excessive Multicollinearity

The presence of high levels of multicollinearity could make individual coefficients of the exchange rate variables appear to be non-significant when they are in fact significant. In order to determine the extent to which the results were threatened by the presence of high levels of multicollinearity a test for the detection of its presence was conducted.

The variance inflation factor (VIF) is often used to detect excessive multicollinearity and it was computed in the present study. The formula for the calculation of the VIF is as follows:

$$VIF = 1/(1-R^2_k)$$

Where R^2_k = the coefficient of determination in the least squares
regression with the kth explanatory variable as the
"dependent" variable and all the remainng explanatory
variables as regressors.

In the pass-through measurement model outlined above this would mean
that each of the lags of the exchange rate variable was regressed against
all of the other lags in order to obtain R^2_k. The VIF then becomes an
indication of the extent to which the collinearity between the
coefficients is causing their variances to be inflated. The higher the
degree of multicollinearity, the higher the value of the VIF will be.

Tests for Statistical Significance of Pass-Through

Aside from the traditional t-tests for significance of the
individual coefficients of the exchange rate variable and its lags, two F-
tests were also performed. One F-statistic tested the null hypothesis that
the *sum* of the coefficients of the contemporaneous value of the
exchange rate variable and its twelve monthly lags was zero. If the F-
statistic were statistically significant the null hypothesis would be
rejected and one would conclude that the pass-through rate (or the sum
of the coefficients of the exchange rate variable and its lags) was not
zero. The other F-statistic was used to test the null hypothesis that all
individual regression coefficients were equal to zero. Since pass-through
is defined as the sum of the coefficients of the contemporaneous and
lagged values of the exchange variable, the F-test of the sum of the
coefficients was the most vital.

The testing of the sum of the coefficients rather than relying
on t-tests of individual coefficients also has the advantage of reducing
the problems mentioned above that could be introduced by the presence
of multicollinearity between the contemporaneous and lagged values of
the exchange rate variable. This is not a problem when testing a
hypothesis involving the sum of these coefficients as the above-
described F-test does.

RESULTS

In this section the results of the regression-based measurement
model analyses are reported. The results reported are those of the

general distributed lag model. The use of the Prais-Winsten transformation for dealing with excessive serial correlation is discussed as are the results of the tests for detection of multicollinearity.

Results of the General Distributed Lag Model

Of the 258 product/country combinations that were analyzed using the general model there was only one that demonstrated a statistically significant rate of pass-through at the .05 level for the entire time span of the sample (1979-1988) when using the above-described F-test to determine the statistical significance of the pass-through measure (the sum of the coefficients of the lags of the exchange rate variable). This lone combination was beer imported from the Netherlands.

The overall pass-through rate for Dutch beer across the entire time span of the sample was .75 or 75 percent. This particular product/country combination also demonstrated a significant level of pass-through for both sub-periods of Dutch guilder appreciation/ depreciation. As the guilder generally depreciated against the U.S. dollar from January of 1979 through March of 1985 the rate of pass-through was 65 percent. As the guilder appreciated from April of 1985 through the end of the sample period in December of 1988 the pass-through rate was 96 percent. This means that the price behavior of Dutch beer imported into the U.S. during this period was virtually identical to the behavior of the guilder/dollar exchange rate.

The comparability of the behavior of these two time series is graphically demonstrated by Figure 7.3. It is evident that the changes in the import price and the changes in the guilder/dollar exchange rate are moving in concert.

One other product/country combination demonstrated a significant level of pass-through at the .05 level for a sub-period of the sample. Six-cylinder automobiles from Japan demonstrated a pass-through rate of 77 percent for the sub-period of November 1982 through June 1987. The period of November 1982 through September 1985 was one of minor fluctuations in the yen/dollar exchange rate. The period from October 1985 through June 1987 witnessed a tremendous appreciation in the value of the yen. The sample frame of this product was ended in June 1987 because the unit values were very erratic beginning in July 1987. The unit values began to behave erratically

FIGURE 7.3

DUTCH BEER PRICES AND THE GUILDER/U.S. DOLLAR EXCHANGE RATE: 1978-1988

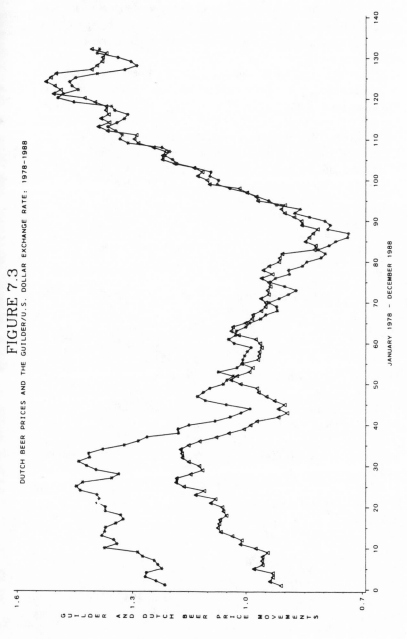

JANUARY 1978 - DECEMBER 1988

GUILDER=*   DUTCH BEER PRICES=TRIANGLE

about the time that Japanese auto manufacturers launched their luxury models with six-cylinder engines. This change in the composition of auto imports was a potential cause of this erratic behavior in unit values.

When the level of significance for the F-test was increased to the .10 level there were eight product/country combinations added to the two mentioned above. For six of these combinations the rate of pass-through was significant for the overall time period of the sample. One of these six also demonstrated a significant level of pass-through for one sub-period. Two additional combinations demonstrated significant levels of pass-through for one sub-period of either currency appreciation or depreciation. These results are detailed below in Table 7.2.

Table 7.2

Product/Country Combinations Demonstrating Significant
Positive Levels of Pass-Through

TSUSA #	Product Description	PT Rate	Time Period	Country
1670515*	Beer	.75	1/79-12/88	Neth.
		.65	1/79-2/85	
		.96	3/85-12/88	
6921015*	6-cylinder autos	.89	10/85-6/87	Japan
1670515	Beer	.14	1/79-12/88	Mexico
6103955	Unalloyed St. Pipe	1.60	1/79-12/88	Canada
6103955	Unalloyed St. Pipe	.57	1/79-12/88	Japan
		.72	1/79-10/82	
6465400	Iron/St. Bolts	.90	1/79-12/88	Japan
6465600	Iron/St. Nuts	.97	1/79-12/88	Japan
6921030#	8-cylinder autos	.93	1/79-11/85	W.Ger.
6923402	Ag Trac. < 20HP	2.21	1/80-10/82	Japan
7321800	Bicycles, 25-36" under $16.66	2.07	1/79-10/82	Japan

* Significant at .05 level. All others significant at .10.
# For 8-cylinder autos from Germany the time frame is January 1979 through November of 1985. After November of 1985 the behavior of the unit values of this category became erratic, indicating heterogeneity of the category.

There was one additional combination whose pass-through rate was shown to be statistically significant. However, the pass-through was negative. Since a negative pass-through rate would indicate that some force other than exchange rates was driving the pricing of this product (leather casual shoes from Hong Kong), it was not reported in Table 7.2. This was the only example of a statistically significant level of pass-through that was negative.

Correcting for Excessive Serial Correlation

The D-W statistics for the unconstrained model often indicated that there was excessive serial correlation present for product/country combinations. However, transforming the measurement model using a Prais-Winsten type formulation for handling problems with excessive serial correlation and re-estimating it did not lead to even a minor change in the fact that very few of the product/country combinations demonstrated statistically significant levels of pass-through. In fact, no combination was added to the list of those demonstrating significant levels of pass-through. The transformation actually led to increases in the standard errors of the regression coefficients of the exchange rate variables in almost every case due to the fact that the serial correlations were negative for the time series. This was the case for all but five of the product/country combinations whose Durbin-Watson statistic indicated that serial correlation was excessive.

Results of Test for Excessive Multicollinearity

Kennedy (1985) suggests that a good rule of thumb is to consider multicollinearity to be a serious problem only when the VIF is greater than 10.0. The only exchange rate series for which the VIF had a value in excess of 1.6 was the Brazilian cruzado at 4.25. These results indicate that problems with inflated standard errors due to multicollinearity were practically non-existent in these data.

An additional method for the detection of excessive multicollinearity is to determine whether the F statistic testing the hypothesis that the sum of the coefficients of the exchange rate lags is significant (indicating that the sum of the coefficients is different from zero) while none of the t statistics for the individual regression coefficients is significant. Such a situation would indicate that the separate influence of each of the explanatory variables (exchange rate lags) is weak relative to their joint influence on the dependent variable (change in import prices). This situation is symptomatic of a high degree of multicollinearity.

There was only one case of a significant F statistic with no significant t statistics at the .05 level in the analysis of the 258 product/country combinations. That combination is reported as having demonstrated a statistically significant level of pass-through (6-cylinder cars from Japan). In fact, as reported in Table 7.2, there were only thirteen cases in which the F statistic was significant at all for either the overall sample or any of the sub-periods that were examined.

The variances of the regression coefficients of the exchange rate variable and its lags were often relatively large in this sample. While this can result from excessive multicollinearity, such large variances of the coefficients of the explanatory variables could also be caused by other problems. These variances may be large because the explanatory variables themselves have a small dispersion as shown for the U.S. Dollar/Canadian Dollar exchange rate in Table 7.1. This lack of dispersion was also the case for the exchange rate variables of other countries, including Taiwan and Singapore. These large variances can also result from the fact that the variance of the overall regression disturbance term (σ^2) itself is large.

The lack of serious problems with multicollinearity is certainly the rule for the lagged first-differences of the exchange rate variable. This finding is certainly comforting since such problems could seriously hamper efforts at interpretation of these regression coefficients. This lack of multicollinearity also implies that there is a lack of serial correlation in the underlying process that generates exchange rates. This would seem to support the notion that exchange rates tend to move in the fashion of a random walk in the short term. Even if multicollinearity had been excessive, the problems of interpretation created by this would have been minimized by the fact that the sum of the regression coefficients, rather than the individual coefficients, was the point of interest in this study.

OTHER POSSIBLE LIMITATIONS OF
THE MEASUREMENT PROCESS

There are several other possible limitations inherent in the pass-through measurement process utilized that should be summarized here. It is obvious that there are variables other than exchange rates that could impact import prices. One is likely production costs.

While the omission of these costs may be a cause for concern when interpreting the results of the measurement model, the problem is somewhat ameliorated by the very nature of the pass-through measurement model itself. Dramatic changes in production costs in the span of one year (the number of lags of the exchange rate variable) seem unlikely for most kinds of products. Relating the changes in import prices to the changes in the explanatory variables for the finite period of one year means that the impact on import prices of changes in the importer's production cost structure should be minimal.

Another concern that arises when examining international pricing behavior is that of transfer pricing. If the "foreign" firm importing into the U.S. is a subsidiary of a U.S. based parent there could be a temptation to transfer products into the U.S. at prices that do not represent a realistic value. This could be due to tax or other types of considerations. This same sort of behavior could be exhibited by a foreign-based firm that has a U.S. marketing division. It could transfer products to this marketing subsidiary at unrealistic prices for numerous reasons. As mentioned above, this potential problem is greatly lessened by the price checking function of the U.S. Bureau of Customs.

This study may also be limited by its failure to attempt to determine whether the risks inherent in exchange rate fluctuations are managed in some fashion by hedging of exchange rate risks in forward markets. It seems possible that a firm could greatly reduce its exposure to such risks by the skillful use of exchange rate hedging. This could explain a lack of pass-through and would not be accounted for by the measurement model.

The problems inherent in the necessity of using unit values as proxies for import prices have been alluded to previously. The use of such a questionable surrogate for a key variable could be driving the results in some of the country/product combinations. However, it is unlikely that this could be the case for all of the products in the type of broad-based sample that was used in the present study.

Finally, some of the assumptions inherent in the model could also limit its usefulness. The use of a partial equilibrium model in which exchange rates are assumed to be exogenous could be troublesome. However, the development of a more complete model that includes exchange rates as an endogenous variable does not seem necessary for the present research.

The use of actual, rather than expected, exchange rates could also be problematic. The use of actual exchange rates somewhat implies that foreign exchange markets are efficient. Such a rational expectations approach may not be representative of reality and this may call for the use of some form of expected value of the exchange rate in future research.

Finally, the use of a non-recursive model in which it is assumed that there is a uni-directional path running from exchange rates to import prices may also be somewhat unrealistic. However, this does not seem to be inappropriate for a study of the present type, especially in light of the empirical findings discussed above in which Kenen and Pack (1980) found that the impact of import prices on exchange rates is not significant.

SUPPLEMENTAL ANALYSES

To assure that the above-reported results of the general distributed lag model were not driven by the choice of lag structures, two supplemental analyses were performed. Pass-through was measured with an additional regression-based model utilizing an alternative distributed lag structure (second-degree PDL) and with the end-point method.

Second-Degree PDL Structure

To minimize the possibility that the pass-through measurements generated by the general distributed lag model were driven by the choice of this particular lag structure, an additional distributed lag measurement model was analyzed. Even though Cassidy (1981) and others have warned against the use of constraints such as those imposed on regression coefficients by PDL models, the supplemental model chosen was a second-degree PDL. This choice was motivated by the fact that some of the earlier empirical pass-through studies had utilized this type of model in their pass-through measurements (see Table 2.1).

To formulate a PDL model the researcher must specify the appropriate degree of the polynomial and state the number of periods before the weights associated with the coefficients of the lagged variable can be assumed to be zero, that is the model must be made finite by limiting the number of lags to be included as explanatory variables. To make each of these weights $w_0, w_1, \ldots, w_n$ lie along a second-degree polynomial curve, we specify that:

$$w_i = \lambda_0 + \lambda_1 i + \lambda_2 i^2 \qquad (i = 0, 1, 2, \ldots, n).$$

Some researchers add the further restrictions that $w_{-1} = 0$ and $w_{n+1} = 0$. These restrictions are known as end-point restrictions. Kmenta (1986) recommends against their use because the model to be estimated involves only the weights $w_0, w_1, \ldots, w_n$ and gives no information on the behavior of the polynomial outside of this range. The second-degree polynomial lag model to be estimated without end-point restrictions then becomes:

$$\Delta lnIP_t = \alpha + \beta[\lambda_0 \Delta lnFX_t + (\lambda_0 + \lambda_1 + \lambda_2)\Delta lnFX_{t-1} + (\lambda_0 + 2\lambda_1 + 2^2\lambda_2)\Delta lnFX_{t-2} + \ldots + (\lambda_0 + 12\lambda_1 + 12^2\lambda_2)\Delta lnFX_{t-12} + e_t$$

Where $\Delta lnIP_t$ = change in the natural logarithm of the
     Import Price from previous month

   $\Delta lnFX_t$ = change in the log of the exchange rate

   α = intercept term

   β = matrix of coefficient weights for the contemporaneous
     and 12 monthly lags of the exchange rate variable

   e_t = error term

   Pass-Through = $\Sigma\beta$

While I am still uncomfortable with the imposition of a polynomial constraint, the computer program utilized for analyzing this model (PROC PDLREG in SAS) reports a t-statistic for the second-degree constraint. If the t-statistic is not significant the implication is that the use of the constraint is not appropriate for the data being analyzed. The t-test demonstrated that the polynomial constraint was appropriate for only 17 of the 258 product/country combinations.

Detailed results of this formulation of a pass-through measurement model are presented in Appendix D. Only those product/country combinations for which the second degree polynomial constraint was found to be appropriate are reported in the appendix. However, there were only four combinations not reported for this reason that had more than one significant coefficient of the exchange rate variable or any of its twelve lags.

End-Point Analysis

The results of the end-point method of measuring pass-through are presented in Appendix E. Measurements for all 258 product/country combinations are presented for both the overall time frame of the sample and for sub-periods of exchange rate appreciation and depreciation. The reader should also note that for Japan and Hong Kong there was one period during which exchange rates were basically stable.

The formula used in the end-point calculation is as follows:

Pass-Through = $[(IP_E - IP_B)/IP_B]/[(FX_E - FX_B)/FX_B]$

Where IP_E = Import price at the end of the time period.
IP_B = Import price at the beginning of the time period.
FX_E = Exchange rate at the end of the time period.
FX_B = Exchange rate at the beginning of the time period.

This could also be written as:

Pass-Through = %ΔImport Price/%ΔExchange Rate.

This formulation implies that for a positive relationship to exist between changes in import prices and changes in exchange rates the end-point pass-through rate would be positive. Negative pass-through rates would mean that an appreciation of a foreign currency against the U.S. dollar would be associated with a decrease in the U.S. dollar price of products imported into the U.S. from that country (e.g., a yen appreciation is associated with a lowering of the U.S. prices of Japanese imports). A pass-through rate between zero and one would mean that a less-than-proportional response of import prices to exchange rate changes had occured.

THE ANALYSIS OF SELECTED ADDITIONAL PRODUCTS

The failure of certain products to meet the sample selection criteria caused them to be selectively added to the sample of product/country combinations to be analyzed. The reason for adding this group of products was that they are examples of products that have received much attention from sources such as the popular business press and governmental agencies in the ongoing debate concerning fair trade.

These products are: (1) motorcycles from Japan, (2) two categories of textile products coming from Hong Kong, the Philippines, South Korea, and Taiwan, and (3) 35 mm still cameras from Japan and Taiwan. Unit value data were gathered from U.S. Department of Commerce data on imports reported on a monthly basis under the U.N.-based 7-digit SITC classification. This data source was more readily available than the 7-digit TSUSA data for the hand-gathering of data and the SITC categories for these products were very similar to the comparable TSUSA categories.

The results were little different from those for the bulk of the product/country combinations included in the original sample. Of the seven product/country combinations included in this supplemental sample, only one demonstrated any statistically significant level of pass-through. Cameras from Japan demonstrated pass-through at the rate of 124 percent for the overall time period. None of the sub-periods demonstrated pass-through for any of the combinations.

THE SPECIAL "CASE" OF DUTCH BEER

The finding that only one product/country combination had an almost perfect relationship between movements in import prices and exchange rates made this a very unique and interesting case. When it became evident that beer imported into the U.S. from the Netherlands was such a special product in this regard the decision was made to investigate in some greater degree of detail.

The first step of this investigation was to determine the appropriate person(s) to contact to discuss this phenomenon. The U.S. distributor of Heineken beer products in New York City was contacted. Information obtained from this source indicated that almost 100 percent of the Dutch beer imported to the U.S. during the period of the sample was brewed by Heineken.

The decision was made to contact Heineken at its corporate headquarters in Amsterdam. The U.S. distributor in New York City (who has distribution rights for the entire U.S.) gave me the fax number to call at Heineken's export department in Amsterdam. Heineken's Director of Export responded to my inquiry and indicated that the reason for the close relationship between Heineken prices in the U.S. in dollars and the guilder/dollar exchange rate was simple: Heineken prices its product in guilders. They apparently are not overly concerned with attempting to anticipate the impact that such a cost-based pricing strategy might have on U.S. sales.

Heineken is apparently convinced that they have successfully differentiated their product in the U.S. market and will not lose much (if any) market share as a result of adopting such a strategy (they might anticipate losing market share only when the guilder was increasing in value against the U.S. dollar and the result was higher U.S. dollar prices because movement in the opposite direction would cause the price in U.S. dollars to decrease and the effect on Heineken's U.S. market share should be positive). This sort of strategy is what one would expect if businesspeople reacted to exchange rate fluctuations as some economic theory, such as the law of one price, would tend to indicate. However, the results of the pass-through measurement models presented above make it appear that this sort of reaction is very unusual for firms exporting into the U.S. market.

NOTES

1. The graphical, univariate, correlation, and regression analyses reported in this study were performed using the SAS mainframe statistical package. The specific programs used were PROC SASGRAPH, PROC UNIVARIATE, PROC CORR, PROC REG, PROC AUTOREG, and PROC PDLREG. Refer to the *SAS User's Guide: Basics*, Version 5 edition, 1985, the *SAS User's Guide: Statistics*, Version 5, 1985, and *SAS/ETS User's Guide*, Version 6, First edition, 1988, all published by the SAS Institute, Inc., Cary, NC, for specific information regarding these programs.

2. This Prais-Winsten transformation was accomplished utilizing PROC AUTOREG in SAS as explained in *SAS/ETS User's Guide*, Version 6, First edition, SAS Institute, Inc., Cary, NC, 1988.

VIII

Conclusions

In this chapter the results of the above-reported analyses will be interpreted by the author, some ramifications that the findings might have for theory development in international pricing will be considered, potential managerial implications of these findings will be discussed, various directions that may be taken in future research on this general topic, including data needs, will be contemplated, a summary of the study and its major findings will be offered, and some concluding remarks will be made.

INTERPRETATION OF MEASUREMENT MODEL RESULTS

The most striking result of the analysis of the pass-through measurement model was the failure of most product/country combinations to demonstrate any statistically significant rate of pass-through at the .05 level. This finding held true regardless of the distributed lag formulation of the measurement model as the number of product/country combinations that demonstrated a statistically significant level of pass-through was little different under the two distributed lag-structures that were tested. Even the addition of product/country combinations that had statistically significant levels of pass-through at the .10 level did not dramatically increase the total number of combinations demonstrating pass-through.

General Conclusions Concerning Pass-Through

The overall conclusion must be that a zero (or near zero) rate of pass-through was the rule rather than the exception in this particular sample regardless of the type of lag structure utilized. One must also conclude that even when pass-through does occur it is usually something less than one hundred percent.

Time Lag of Pass-Through Response

The present study does seem to verify earlier empirical work on pass-through that found that any adjustment of import prices to exchange rate fluctuations does take place over some period of time rather than instantaneously. As mentioned above, such behavior could be explained in several ways. For example, a model of adaptive expectations could be appropriate as foreign producers respond incrementally in their attempts to determine whether the "new" exchange rate will tend to become permanent or is just an aberration. One should also remember that any conclusions should be made with great care when such a small number of cases with any kind of pass-through behavior exists.

Asymmetry of Pass-Through Response

For the limited number of combinations demonstrating pass-through one would conclude that there is no compelling case that argues for asymmetry. The results of the distributed lag regression models (as seen in Table 7.2) do not indicate that the pricing reaction to exchange rate depreciations is different from that of appreciations. The number of combinations with pass-through in periods of appreciation is not greatly different from the number during periods of depreciation.

Pass-Through According to Product-Type

Of the ten product/country combinations demonstrating some statistically significant level of pass-through under the general distributed lag measurement model (see Table 7.2), two were consumer non-durables, three were consumer durables, one was a capital good, and four were intermediate goods. It is difficult to establish any sort of pattern according to product-type with this small number of observations.

Of the fifteen combinations demonstrating positive pass-through using the second-degree PDL model, three were consumer non-durables, four were consumer durables, one was a capital good, and seven were intermediate goods. The only tentative conclusions that could be drawn from these models are: (1) there could be a tendency for pass-through to be more prevalent for intermediate goods than other product types, and (2) there could be a tendency for pass-through to be less prevalent for capital goods than for other product types.

These weak conclusions could indicate that the profit margins of products have an impact on the likelihood of pass-through occurring. The profit margins on intermediate goods could be somewhat lower than those for other product types that may be more amenable to product differentiation. This would mean that the failure to pass-through could quickly put a foreign firm in a loss position. The higher margins that could be involved in the sale of capital goods could allow the absorption of a much greater amount of an exchange rate change prior to dictating a change in pricing of the product.

Country-Specific Pass-Through Behavior

Of the ten product/country combinations that demonstrated a statistically significant level of pass-through under the general distributed lag model, six were from Japan. No other country in the sample had more than one combination that demonstrated pass-through.

Fifteen combinations demonstrated positive pass-through using the second-degree PDL model. Of these fifteen, Japan and Canada had three each, while the United Kingdom and South Korea had two each. No other country had more than one combination demonstrating pass-through.

As with most issues that were raised in this project, the small number of combinations demonstrating pass-through makes addressing this issue very difficult. The only tenuous conclusion ventured here is that for this particular sample, Japan seems to demonstrate more of a willingness to engage in pass-through for its exports to the U.S. than the other countries included in the sample. This would seem to indicate that Japan is certainly no worse about failing to pass-through, and is, if anything, more likely to pass-through than other foreign competitors. However, this conclusion is overwhelmed by the general conclusion that pass-through was not found for the great majority of product/country combinations, including those from Japan.

INTERPRETATION OF END-POINT
MEASUREMENT RESULTS

As mentioned above, the end-point method for measuring pass-through is subject to serious limitations which make this the weakest test of pass-through behavior. The choice of end-points will determine what the pass-through is and this choice is arbitrary. Sometimes a change of one monthly observation can make a substantial difference in the pass-through rate. With this caveat in mind, there are some observations that can be made with respect to the results of the end-point measurement of pass-through.

General Conclusions Concerning Pass-Through

A simple examination of the proportion of products from each country that demonstrated a positive pass-through of at least fifty percent was conducted. Only positive rates of pass-through were included because a negative rate would indicate that U.S. dollar prices of imports decreased as the dollar depreciated and vice-versa. Such a relationship does not seem likely for relatively short-term periods of time (e.g. three years or less). A negative relationship does not seem so unlikely over the entire ten year span of the sample, and while not reported in Appendix E, such negative relationships were quite common for the long-term. Improvements in efficiency of production and other factors could make such a relationship possible over extended periods of time.

The fifty percent rate of pass-through was chosen as an indicator that a substantial level of pass-through had occurred. Some level of pass-through will always occur when the end-point method is used for measurement and the fifty percent cutoff point was arbitrarily chosen to eliminate those products where dramatic responses of import prices to exchange rate changes were not experienced.

With the above criteria used as cutoffs, the proportions of products found to demonstrate pass-through on a country-by-country basis for those countries that had sub-periods of appreciation and depreciation and at least five products in each sub-period are reported in Table 8.1.

Table 8.1

Proportion of Products By Country Demonstrating
Pass-Through Under the End-Point Measurement Method

Japan				
Depreciation 10/78-4/80	Appreciation 4/80-1/81	Depreciation 1/81-10/82	Flat 10/82-9/85	Appreciation 9/85-12/88
8/41=.195	18/42=.429	13/46=.283	15/52=.288	19/54=.352

Taiwan		
Appreciation 1/78-9/79	Depreciation 9/79-9/83	Appreciation 9/83-12/88
19/27=.704	12/36=.333	26/39=.667

Korea	
Depreciation 1/80-9/85	Appreciation 9/85-12/88
10/28=.357	13/32=.406

Canada	
Depreciation 1/78-1/86	Appreciation 1/86-12/88
7/20=.35	10/20=.50

Table 8.1 (continued)
W. Germany

Appreciation 1/78-1/80	Depreciation 1/80-3/85	Appreciation 3/85-12/88
9/12=.75	5/17=.294	9/17=.529

Hong Kong

Depreciation 1/78-9/83	Flat 9/83-12/88	Appreciation 5/86-4/87
2/8=.25	7/10=.70	6/10=.60

United Kingdom

Appreciation 1/78-1/81	Depreciation 1/81-3/85	Appreciation 3/85-12/88
4/5=.80	2/7=.286	5/9=.556

Italy

Appreciation 1/78-1/80	Depreciation 1/80-3/85	Appreciation 3/85-12/88
5/7=.714	1/8=.125	3/8=.375

Singapore

Appreciation 1/78-12/81	Depreciation 12/81-2/85	Appreciation 2/85-12/88
4/5=.80	6/6=1.00	2/7=.286

It is obvious from an examination of Table 8.1 and Appendix E that the proportion of product/country combinations demonstrating pass-through is much higher for the end-point method than for the regression based time-series methods. One must remember, however, that the end-point measurement method will always demonstrate some level of pass-through due to its construction. It is also obvious that even the end-point method indicates that substantial levels of pass-through (fifty percent or greater) are still the exception rather than the rule. Of the 258 product/country combinations examined with this method, 154 demonstrated pass-through rates below 50 percent for the most recent sub-period of exchange rate movement.

Time Lag of Pass-Through Response

The end-point method is not an examination of a time series. This means that there will be no lag structure to the end-point measurement model and the lag issue is not relevant when using this measure of pass-through.

Asymmetry of Pass-Through Response

The results of the end-point measurement model do seem to indicate that there is a greater likelihood of pass-through occurring during periods of appreciation of foreign currencies then in periods of their depreciation. This indication that during periods of depreciation of foreign currencies, when pass-through would lead to lower dollar prices in the U.S. market, foreign producers were not passing through may be somewhat surprising when one considers the ramifications of a price reduction for the foreign producer's U.S. market share. However, earlier expressed caveats concerning the end-point method make any conclusions based on its results somewhat questionable.

A final observation on sub-periods deals with the trend in pass-through. If periods of appreciation of foreign currencies are compared, it becomes obvious that the proportion of products demonstrating substantial levels of pass-through is decreasing over time. This is demonstrated by Table 8.2 in which the proportion of products demonstrating a fifty percent or higher positive rate of pass-through for those countries with five or more products in each sub-period of appreciation are shown.

Table 8.2

Proportion of Products Demonstrating End-Point
Pass-Through for Periods of Foreign Currency Appreciation

	Initial Appreciation	Final Appreciation
Japan	.429	.352
Taiwan	.704	.667
W. Germany	.750	.529
U.K.	.800	.556
Italy	.714	.375
Singapore	.800	.286
France	1.000	.143

This is a weak indication that foreign competitors in the U.S. market are becoming less likely to pass-through appreciations of their currencies in the form of higher dollar prices in the U.S. market.

Pass-Through According to Product-Type

Of the 104 product/country combinations with end-point pass-through rates that were positive and exceeded fifty percent during the most recent sub-period of exchange rate movement (see Appendix E), 36 were consumer non-durables, 27 were consumer durables, 33 were intermediate goods, and 8 were capital goods. This small number of capital goods somewhat reinforces the results of the regression-based measurement models and may be an indication that the profit margins on these products are wide enough to allow for the absorption of fairly wide exchange rate fluctuations.

Country-Specific Pass-Through Behavior

The wide range in the proportion of products demonstrating positive rates of pass-through in excess of fifty percent during the most recent period of exchange rate change (see Table 8.1) makes any conclusion on the issue of country-specific pass-through behavior questionable. While two-thirds of the combinations from Taiwan demonstrated this sort of pass-through behavior, only about one-third of the combinations from Japan did so. The weakness of the end-point measurement model has caused the present author to refrain from drawing any substantial conclusions from the end-point data on this issue.

IMPLICATIONS FOR THEORY DEVELOPMENT

There would seem to be implications to be drawn by those interested in advancing international pricing theory. The most obvious conclusion is that in the case of a large and important consuming country such as the U.S., any notion that a pricing model which assumes perfectly competitive markets should be seriously questioned. It appears that such models should be founded on an assumption of imperfectly competitive markets. It seems clear from the present study that discriminatory pricing across markets is a very common practice in today's era of floating exchange rates and that the law of one price is simply not realistic on a product-by-product basis.

One could also imply that even in situations where a foreign firm has some market power (e.g., the ability to successfully differentiate its product), there is no certainty that the firm will use this power by extracting the maximum price. Thus, an assumption of profit maximization in the short run is questionable.

As suggested in Chapter 3, the present study has served as a tentative test of Krugman's PTM hypothesis. The almost complete failure to demonstrate that foreign firms pass-through exchange rate fluctuations to individual products when selling into the U.S. market provides at least weak support of the basic contention of this hypothesis in the limited context of the U.S. market (as explained above, there are reasons to expect incomplete pass-through that are independent of the factors outlined by Krugman in the PTM hypothesis). The PTM hypothesis being supported in this study implies that in the U.S. market foreign producers have decided to follow a market-based, rather than a cost-based, pricing strategy. Any attempt at refining international pricing theory must make some accommodation for such findings.

MANAGERIAL IMPLICATIONS OF THE FINDINGS

It should first be mentioned that any implications to be drawn from this study may not be generalizable to non-U.S. settings. Since only U.S. imports are examined, it would be unwise for non-U.S. managers to assume that the findings of the study would be applicable in other markets.

For U.S. managers who are involved in industries producing one of the products specifically included in this study there are immediate implications to be drawn. Since a great majority of the product categories examined failed to demonstrate any statistically significant level of pass-through, the manager would have to conclude that his foreign competitors are not going to respond to exchange rate fluctuations. This is of major importance in pricing decisions and could even lead to a firm's management beginning an inquiry into whether certain foreign competitors are engaging in dumping.

Knowledge of this sort of market-based pricing behavior could also allow U.S. firms to be better prepared to attain their own advantage when the U.S. dollar depreciates. If foreign firms do not pass-through the appreciation of their currencies in the form of higher dollar prices in the U.S., they must have reduced their profit margins. The U.S. competitors could decide to make the foreign firms' positions even more unpleasant by reducing their own prices in the U.S. market. This could eventually lead to the withdrawal of some foreign competitors from the U.S. market.

Managers involved in industries whose products were not represented in the sample or whose products demonstrated some measure of pass-through should also draw some implications from the study. Managers of unrepresented products should anticipate the likelihood that their competitors might also engage in the sort of market-based price behavior that tends to ignore exchange rate fluctuations. Managers in those industries where foreign competitors do pass-through to some extent should be better prepared to anticipate such reactions to exchange rate movements and respond appropriately.

Another implication of these results is that U.S. firms might want to emulate their foreign competitors when attempting to sell their products in foreign markets. The adoption of some sort of market-based pricing strategy might be well advised for important, competitive markets. Such a strategy seems to have worked well for some foreign producers such as the Japanese in the U.S. market in terms of achieving market penetration.

The principal implication of these findings for managers of non-U.S. firms would seem to be that they should be prepared to adopt a market-based pricing strategy for their products sold in the U.S. If they feel that are not in a position to adopt such a strategy they might consider avoiding such a highly competitive market.

DIRECTIONS FOR FUTURE RESEARCH

As mentioned above, Aaker and Day (1986) indicate that two of the goals of exploratory research are to: (1) establish priorities among the research questions that could be raised, that is to determine the "right questions to ask," and (2) learn about the practical problems of carrying out research on the question.

Generalizability Issue

There is clearly a need for continued research in the vein of the present inquiry. The first priority must be to conduct this sort of micro-level examination of pass-through behavior for countries other than the United States. There is no other market in the world with the sheer size or numerous other characteristics that make the U.S. market so unique. It is possible that this very uniqueness could be the principal reason that many U.S. importers do not demonstrate pass-through behavior. This lack of generalizability of the present findings is particularly troublesome and should be addressed early in this stream of research.

Data on Prices of Traded Goods

The practical problem in pass-through research that presents the greatest challenge is the poor quality of available data on important variables. Future research should attempt to gather actual pricing data from international firms rather than relying on a proxy for price such as a product's unit value. While it will likely be difficult to convince firms to divulge pricing information, the rewards to researchers of obtaining such data would be immense.

The availability of pricing data would not only solve the problem of having to substitute unit values for prices but would also reduce problems with institutional reporting and other types of lags inherent in the secondary pricing data available today. It could even be possible for some institution to launch an effort at building a large data base of prices of internationally traded goods. This would be useful for many kinds of international research.

The present research has clearly demonstrated that even the finest level of aggregation of presently available secondary data on traded good prices is inadequate for studying the pass-through phenomenon. The 7-digit TSUSA classification is still so broad in many product categories that the necessity of using unit values as surrogates for import prices severely weakens the quality of the research and limits the conclusions that can safely be drawn from research findings.

The Use of Survey Methods

Another possible approach to dealing with the apprehension of firms to divulge pricing behavior would be to design a study that would utilize the survey method and inquire directly about pass-through behaviors and policies of specific firms. This approach would simply ask about the firm's past behavior in response to exchange rate fluctuations and whether they have developed general policies or procedures for dealing with the pass-through issue. Specific product pricing information would be an asset to any study of the pass-through phenomenon but would not be essential in this type of research design.

Data on Exchange Rates

Another refinement to the approach utilized in the present study could benefit future research. Future projects could utilize some sort of exchange rate expectation rather than actual exchange rates in order to determine whether this sort of exchange rate variable would be more suitable. This might better reflect reality as businesspeople could be basing their pricing actions on their "anticipated" value of the exchange rate at some future date.

Other Marketing Management Issues

If future research were to demonstrate that the findings of the present study were limited to the unique situation of the U.S. market and that most firms do pass-through exchange rate changes in the form of price changes in their international markets, other areas of inquiry would be in order. If differences in pass-through behavior are found across numerous products and markets, the next step would be to attempt to explain these differences. Some of the possible factors that might explain such differences were discussed in the present study. For example, different countries could engage in systematically different pricing behavior, pass-through might vary according to product-type, the timing of pass-through could vary according to several factors, and pass-through behavior could be asymmetrical in nature *vis-a-vis* exchange rate appreciations and depreciations. These questions could certainly be examined further if future studies found sufficient numbers of products that demonstrated pass-through.

In addition to these issues, other questions not addressed in the present study could be examined. The industrial organization literature offers potential for development of hypotheses in pass-through research. As mentioned above, there are several elements of market structure that have been examined in previous research on pass-through. However, none of these studies has utilized micro level data. An examination of the impact of the extent of market domination by sellers, and the extent of product differentiation on pass-through behavior should prove interesting in future studies if pass-through is found to be a common occurrence.

Two concepts emanating from strategic marketing have also received a great deal of attention in discussions of market imperfections. Market share and market growth rate would seem to have potential for explaining differences in pass-through behavior across products. When a competitor has invested much time and other resources into building its share in a foreign market, it may well be reluctant to give up that market share due to exchange rate fluctuations and may choose to maintain its share by keeping its products priced at the market.

Market growth rate could well affect pass-through behavior as a competitor might want to establish as dominant a position as possible in a high-growth market by engaging in price competition to achieve this position. This could include systematically holding the line on price increases that would normally be dictated by an appreciation of the producer's home country currency, that is, utilizing low or zero rates of pass-through.

It is also possible that there will be an interaction between a firm's market share and the industry's growth rate. One would suspect, for instance, that pass-through for a competitor with a small share of a low-growth market might be rather high due to a lack of concern about the long-term strategic impact of such a practice. The competitor with a small share in a high-growth might be expected to be price competitive and choose to engage in lower rates of pass-through (at least in periods of U.S. dollar depreciation) in order to increase share. Product portfolio theory also points to the likelihood of such an interaction as it indicates that different marketing strategies are appropriate for different combinations of market share and market growth rates.

If, on the other hand, the indications of zero pass-through and the incumbent price discrimination across markets are indeed reflective of reality across numerous products and markets, other marketing management issues might arise. An example of such an issue would be how an international sales manager could deal with a situation where price discrimination across various markets served by his firm has resulted from a failure to respond to exchange rate changes. This would afford an advantage to his salespeople located in those markets where prices are effectively lowered while being a distinct disadvantage to those salespeople in the higher-priced markets. The present author has seen this problem raised by an executive involved in international marketing for a U.S. based firm.

SUMMARY OF THE STUDY

The finding that pass-through did not occur for the vast majority of the micro-level products included in the sample utilized in the present study was the major finding. This finding has implications for both academic theoreticians and business practitioners. International pricing theory must be revised so that findings of this sort are accommodated. Managers must be prepared to deal with international competitors who base their prices more on market factors than on cost factors.

Researchers must attempt to find better quality data for use in studies of pass-through. Better data on prices are absolutely essential. They should also attempt to replicate this study in non-U.S. settings.

CONCLUDING COMMENTS

The following quote is representative of comments in the popular business press in regards to the impact that the appreciation of foreign currencies should have on U.S. prices and, more generally, the entire U.S. economy:

> A lower currency carries plenty of costs. Its most widely felt effect will be to make the U.S. poorer. American goods, securities and real estate become cheaper for foreigners, while Americans must work harder and pay more for anything that comes from abroad. The falling dollar also feeds inflation, both by making imports more expensive and by giving U.S. companies more latitude to raise prices. *Fortune*, December 7, 1987, pp. 38-44.

These sorts of expectations about the response of the prices of U.S. imports to a depreciation of the dollar are so prevalent that they are repeated in television news programs and in other media outlets on a regular basis. The present research demonstrates that such comments do not reflect reality and that the prices of U.S. imports, in fact, respond very little, if any, to such changes in the value of the dollar.

Hopefully, the present study will provide future researchers with some useful guidance in the study of some of the issues associated with the response of the prices of internationally traded products to exchange rate fluctuations. If that noble goal is not accomplished, it is hoped that it will at least prevent members of the popular business press from basing their reports on false presumptions.

Appendix A

TSUSA Categories Exceeding $75 Million in Imports - 1988

1004500	1005500	1008500	1061060	1064020	1064040
1073525	1101012	1102045	1103570	1104710	1105250
1107039	1107080	1123420	1144520	1144525	1144530
1144537	1144545	1144557	1144562	1176025	1178855
1212500	1216500	1241025	1304500	1369300	1376000
1454400	1464000	1476100	1476300	1476400	1489820
1561000	1563500	1564000	1571005	1571045	1601020
1602000	1605000	1617720	1651500	1652900	1661000
1670515	1671040	1673030	1673045	1687800	1689600
1691900	1692100	1693800	1702800	1703510	1703520
1761720	1762900	1822000	1823500	1830530	1922400
2008520	2020340	2021540	2021840	2022140	2022740
2024720	2026600	2066000	2069800	2070980	2400320
2401740	2402360	2454720	2500206	2500225	2500267
2500281	2526500	2526725	2526745	2527500	2544620
2544640	2548040	2560500	2568780	2569580	2702580
2705500	2706300	2747560	3063172	3201934	3372055
3385915	3385917	3558100	3601200	3662460	3762430
3765609	3765612	3810240	3810524	3810546	3812430
3814130	3814160	3814770	3815500	3815620	3815650
3816210	3816220	3816240	3817630	3818359	3818360
3818930	3819035	3819400	3819510	3819530	3819540
3819550	3819575	3840505	3840515	3841841	3841880
3842308	3842505	3842815	3842850	3842915	3842950
3843035	3843777	3844614	3844647	3844724	3844765
3844789	3844925	3845251	3845316	3845317	3845697
3846371	3847220	3847877	3847878	3847880	3848012
3848045	3848073	3848245	3849000	3849115	3849152

3849425	3849445	3849936	3849986	3896100	3896270
4011000	4017200	4021600	4053400	4064200	4071910
4081700	4082000	4084180	4102200	4117600	4119500
4120300	4121100	4122250	4154500	4162000	4171240
4210800	4225000	4225220	4239600	4250455	4250620
4252245	4254240	4255290	4278800	4279700	4295320
4295335	4302040	4322800	4373250	4374950	4377600
4380200	4395095	4400000	4453010	4460540	4460576
4461516	4461558	4613500	4614030	4737000	4750510
4750525	4750535	4751010	4751015	4751035	4751505
4751525	4751535	4752528	4752550	4753500	4756510
4756530	4803000	4805000	4806540	4931200	5111440
5137400	5146500	5176100	5201120	5203200	5203300
5203540	5203800	5203900	5211100	5213140	5239160
5322400	5332400	5333000	5336400	5341100	5348700
5349400	5443100	5444120	5462040	5480500	6010600
6012430	6012450	6036200	6050220	6050260	6050270
6052020	6052040	6052060	6057020	6057060	6060900
6061300	6062000	6062400	6063000	6063700	6064400
6066720	6066725	6066735	6067900	6068330	6069700
6071710	6071730	6076610	6076625	6076720	6076730
6078342	6078390	6079020	6079900	6081315	6081325
6081331	6081335	6094125	6098020	6098025	6098045
6103241	6103243	6103258	6103955	6104210	6104969
6120330	6120640	6121020	6130210	6131000	6180200
6180630	6180650	6181000	6181540	6182560	6182563
6200300	6203200	6220200	6240350	6260200	6322000
6403050	6421110	6421500	6440240	6465400	6465600
6466040	6466320	6469210	6470100	6470200	6494915
6517550	6521540	6528400	6528500	6529400	6530000
6532210	6533915	6533925	6535234	6539420	6540045
6542590	6572565	6572580	6572585	6573535	6574080
6604220	6604260	6604850	6604900	6605622	6605624
6605640	6605655	6606100	6606400	6606705	6606719
6606732	6606752	6606800	6607119	6607150	6607160
6607165	6607300	6609200	6609702	6609756	6609760
6610610	6610625	6610638	6610640	6610900	6611018
6611020	6611074	6611500	6612003	6612031	6613505
6613570	6616890	6619580	6621040	6622045	6622050
6622065	6625000	6640710	6640720	6640820	6640830

6640850	6641031	6641056	6641060	6641076	6641081
6660050	6660070	6660075	6662570	6680250	6680270
6680600	6681020	6682100	6682345	6682350	6685060
6700620	6700660	6707410	6707430	6721400	6721620
6722550	6742030	6743506	6743596	6744242	6744249
6745020	6745325	6745385	6747025	6760510	6760700
6761510	6761520	6761530	6762011	6762017	6762200
6762500	6763012	6763016	6763041	6763043	6763046
6763049	6763052	6763055	6763058	6763060	6763065
6763069	6763073	6763077	6763090	6765030	6765417
6765419	6765421	6765423	6765425	6765429	6765431
6765433	6765455	6765630	6765645.	6765650	6765675
6765695	6783517	6783545	6783570	6784520	6784800
6785012	6785059	6785061	6785075	6785097	6801210
6801745	6802727	6802749	6802755	6803708	6803712
6803717	6803960	6804910	6804960	6813900	6820520
6820710	6822540	6823505	6823510	6826048	6826051
6826053	6826055	6826057	6826063	6826070	6826080
6829000	6829500	6831515	6831525	6833250	6835020
6836010	6836040	6836060	6836090	6836500	6839040
6841500	6842020	6842500	6842895	6844805	6844815
6845710	6845730	6845810	6845815	6845825	6845830
6845835	6845940	6846635	6846645	6846700	6847023
6847025	6847027	6847030	6847040	6847050	6849025
6849060	6849252	6849258	6849262	6849263	6849864
6849866	6850000	6850200	6850477	6850479	6850802
6850804	6850806	6850820	6850860	6851215	6851411
6851430	6851457	6852443	6852500	6852805	6852810
6852820	6853162	6853300	6853852	6853905	6854026
6854029	6854052	6854070	6854934	6854974	6854990
6856035	6856060	6856538	6857304	6857320	6857325
6857380	6858001	6858016	6859026	6859034	6859036
6859038	6859054	6859058	6859059	6859080	6859100
6861035	6868040	6869030	6875405	6875408	6877025
6877027	6877255	6877405	6877410	6877415	6877420
6877425	6877430	6877435	6877437	6877441	6877443
6877444	6877445	6877450	6877455	6877460	6877705
6877790	6877900	6878100	6878505	6878520	6880465
6881010	6881020	6881200	6881300	6881800	6883610
6884280	6900500	6904000	6920210	6920310	6920320

6920720	6920740	6921006	6921008	6921011	6921012
6921014	6921015	6921030	6921035	6921040	6921090
6921110	6921115	6921130	6922010	6922052	6922056
6922180	6923140	6923215	6923220	6923230	6923242
6923260	6923262	6923264	6923274	6923276	6923278
6923282	6923288	6923295	6923320	6923330	6923372
6923376	6923390	6923402	6923404	6923406	6923409
6923411	6923430	6923440	6923460	6923534	6924015
6924025	6924030	6924070	6924520	6925230	6925360
6925380	6925500	6926000	6924120	6944125	6944148
6944150	6944160	6944165	6946100	6946110	6946700
6940510	6961004	6961530	7002946	7003522	7003552
7003575	7004505	7004507	7004514	7004544	7004560
7005605	7005610	7005620	7005636	7005646	7005670
7006400	7006700	7009515	7058200	7058300	7060500
7060700	7060900	7061310	7064135	7066225	7066240
7066245	7080140	7082320	7084520	7084720	7085200
7090500	7090940	7091720	7091770	7091790	7092700
7094500	7096320	7096340	7108080	7117820	7124800
7124910	7124950	7124955	7124960	7124971	7124975
7125200	7150509	7150510	7150511	7221100	7221625
7221630	7221640	7229400	7231507	7231565	7231578
7231590	7233030	7233500	7244050	7244510	7244530
7244540	7244560	7244570	7250320	7254765	7254775
7255000	7270600	7270700	7271100	7272900	7273525
7273530	7273535	7273545	7273550	7273555	7273590
7274140	7275900	7277045	7277065	7277080	7301900
7309900	7311520	7312400	7321800	7322400	7325200
7326020	7341500	7342009	7342012	7342040	7347742
7350215	7352052	7352057	7352058	7371400	7371600
7371800	7371900	7373000	7374000	7375500	7379300
7379600	7379865	7401300	7401400	7401500	7403500
7404100	7407000	7410600	7510510	7600520	7650300
7651500	7662540	7662560	7714310	7714312	7714316
7715500	7721600	7722010	7722035	7722045	7723195
7723520	7723550	7725109	7725127	7725136	7725138
7725146	7728500	7729700	7732500	7745800	7747000
7903900	7911520	7911540	7912700	7916000	7917620
7917640	7917660	8000035	8010000	8062040	9999500

Appendix B

Listing of Product Categories Studied

TSUSA #	Brief Product Description	Major U.S. Importers
1563500	Cocoa Butter	Brazil, Malaysia, Mexico, Singapore
1602000	Soluble or Instant Coffee	Brazil
1670515	Beer	Canada, Germany, Mexico, Netherlands
2527500	Writing Paper	Brazil, Canada, Mexico
2560500	Wall Paper	Canada, Germany, Italy, Korea, U.K.
3558100	Woven or knit Fabric, 70% rubber or plastic	Canada, Taiwan
3762430	Bras	Mexico, Philippines
4011000	Benzene	Canada, Japan
4017200	Toulene	Canada, Japan
4210800	Sodium Hydroxide	Canada
4225220	Uranium Fluorides	Canada
4460540	Rubber milk or latex	Malaysia
4461516	Polybutadiene rubber	Canada, Japan, Mexico
4613500	Perfume, cologne, etc.	France
4737000	Titanium dioxide	Canada, France, Germany, U.K.
5176100	Electrodes, partially carbon or graphite	Japan
6103955	Steel pipe, unalloyed, welded, not casing	Canada, Japan, Singapore
6421110	Steel wire strand, brass plated	Germany, Italy, Japan, Spain
6465400	Bolts, bolts and nut	Canada, Japan, Taiwan
6465600	Nuts of iron or steel	Japan, Taiwan

TSUSA #	Brief Product Description	Major U.S.Importers
6466320	Cap screw with diameter over 24 inches	Canada, Japan, Taiwan
6604260	Piston-type diesel engine, excluding auto and mfg.	Japan
6604850	Piston-type auto., truck and bus engine, exclud. diesel	Germany, Japan, Mexico
6609702	Motor vehicle pumps, liquid	Germany, U.K.
6610610	Electric fans, excluding permanently installed	Taiwan
6610900	Air cond. & refrig. compres., 1/4 hp or less	Brazil, Italy, Singapore
6611020	Air cond. & refrig. compres., over 1/4 hp, not over 1 hp	Japan
6613505	Refrigerator and refrig. freezer, under 6.5 cu. ft.	Korea, Mexico
6640720	Wheel-type front-end loaders	Canada, Japan
6640820	Track-type front-end loaders	France
6641056	Hydraulic jacks	Taiwan
6747025	Chainsaws	Germany, Japan, Sweden
6760510	Portable typewriter, elec., not automatic, no calcula.	Japan, Singapore
6762011	Electronic hand-held or pocket calculator	Hong Kong, Japan, Taiwan
6763012	Electrostatic copy machine, indirect process	Japan
6763016	Photocopying machines, not specifically provided for	Japan, Netherlands
6822540	Electric motors, under 1/40 hp, dc	Hong Kong, Japan Taiwan
6823505	Electric motors, over 1/10 but under 1 hp, ac	Mexico
6823510	Electric motors, over 1/10 but under 1 hp, dc	Canada, Mexico
6835020	Shavers with self-contained electric motor	Netherlands
6836010	Battery charging generators and alternators	Germany, Japan, Korea, Mexico
6836040	Starting motors	Germany, Japan
6836060	Spark plugs	Germany, Japan

TSUSA #	Brief Product Description	Major U.S. Importers
6842020	Coffee makers	Germany, Hong Kong
6842500	Microwave ovens	Japan, Korea, Singapore
6844805	Electric hair dryers	Hong Kong, Taiwan
6847023	Loudspeaker with a single speaker, not enclosed	Japan, Korea, Taiwan
6847025	Loudspeakers, multiple multi-speaker type	Japan, Taiwan
6847030	Audio-frequency elec. amp.	Japan, Korea, Taiwan
6849252	13 inch color TV's	Korea, Malaysia, Mexico, Singapore, Taiwan
6849258	18 and 19 inch color TV's	Korea, Mexico, Taiwan
6850200	Tuners for TV receivers	Malaysia, Taiwan
6851215	AM/FM solid state, broad band radio receivers for motor vehicle installation	Brazil, Japan, Mexico
6851430	Stereo radio without speakers, excluding battery operated	Japan
6853905	Telephone announce and record machines	Hong Kong, Japan, Korea, Singapore
6854052	VCR's	Japan, Korea, Taiwan
6859026	Snap-action switches	Mexico
6859034	Relays with contacts under 10 amps	Japan, Mexico
6859036	Relays with contacts over 10 amps	Germany, Japan
6869030	Household and other lamps	Korea, Taiwan
6880465	Insulated power cable, less than 601 volt capacity	Canada, Mexico, Taiwan
6921014	New 4-cylinder autos other than station wag. & vans	Japan, Korea, Sweden
6921015	Autos over 4 but not over 6 cylinders	Germany, Japan, U.K.
6921030	Autos over 6 cylinders	Germany
6922052	Truck chassis under 19,500 lb., excluding gas	France
6922056	Truck chassis, 26,000 to 33,000 lb.	Brazil, Japan
6923402	Wheel-type agri Tractors, under 20 hp	Japan, U.K.

TSUSA #	Brief Product Description	Major U.S.Importers
6923406	Wheel-type agri Tractors, 40 to 80 hp	Germany, Japan, U.K.
6923409	Wheel-type agri Tractors, 80 to 100 hp	Germany, U.K.
6923430	Track-type agri Trac., new	Japan
6944148	Airplane, non-mil., multi-engine, 4,400 to 10,000 lb.	U.K.
7002946	Leather footwear for work, over $6.80 per pair	Korea, Taiwan
7003522	Leather athletic footwear, male, not specifically provided for	Korea, Taiwan
7003552	Leather footwear for men, cement soles, not specif. provided for	Brazil, Italy, Korea, Spain, Taiwan
7004505	Leather athletic footwear, women & misses, over $2.50	Korea, Taiwan
7004514	Leather casual footwear, women, over $2.50	Brazil, Hong Kong, Taiwan
7004544	Leather footwear, women, cement sole, over $2.50	Brazil, Spain, Taiwan
7005605	Ski boots, uppers 90% rubber or plastic	Italy
7005610	Men's athletic footwear, uppers 90% rubber/plastic	Taiwan
7005620	Women/misses athletic ftwr., uppers 90% rubber/plastic	Korea, Taiwan
7006400	Sneakers with rubber sole affixed and not over $3.00	Korea, Taiwan
7006700	Sneakers with rubber sole, $3.00 to $6.50	Korea, Taiwan
7058200	Seamless rub./plastic gloves	Taiwan
7060500	Leather flat goods, excluding reptile	Italy, Korea
7066225	Handbags of plastics	Korea, Taiwan
7082320	Photographic lenses mounted	Japan, Korea
7084520	Sunglasses over $2.50/dozen	Korea, Taiwan
7084720	Eyeglasses with frames	Italy, Japan
7085200	Prism binoculars	Japan, Korea, Taiwan

TSUSA #	Brief Product Description	Major U.S.Importers
7150509	Watch, 0 to 1 jewel, case of precious metal	Hong Kong, Japan
7231507	Medical x-ray film, unexposed	Japan
7231565	35mm st. film, color, retail	Japan, U.K.
7233030	Silver halide paper for color picture negatives	Brazil, Germany, Japan
7244510	Audio cassettes, blank	Hong Kong, Japan, Korea, Mexico
7244540	Video cassettes, blank	Hong Kong, Japan, Korea
7250320	Grand pianos	Japan, Korea
7255000	Music boxes	Hong Kong, Japan, Taiwan
7301900	Pistols & revolvers over $8.00	Brazil
7311520	Fishing rods	Korea, Taiwan
7312400	Fishing reels, over $8.45	Japan, Korea, Sweden
7321800	Bicycles over 25 in., under 36 in., over $16.66	Japan, Korea, Taiwan
7322400	Bicycles over 25 in., over $16.66, not elsewhere specified	Japan, Korea, Taiwan
7350215	Snow skis	France, Spain
7373000	Stuffed animals over a specific value	Korea, Taiwan
7510510	Hand-held rain umbrellas	Hong Kong, Taiwan
7600520	Ball-point pens and pencils	Japan
7714310	Polyester film, sheets, etc.	Japan, Korea, U.K.
7714312	Pvc film, strips and sheets	Canada, Germany, Japan, Taiwan
7722010	Rubber or plastic bags, etc.	Canada, Taiwan
7725109	New auto tires, radial	Canada, France, Germany, Italy, Japan, Spain
7725136	Other truck and bus tires, radial	Canada, France, Japan
7912700	Shoe uppers, cut leather	Brazil, Mexico

Appendix C

Listing of Products by Product Type

Consumer Non-Durables

TSUSA #	Brief Product Description	1988 Imports in Mil. $
1563500	Cocoa Butter	304
1602000	Soluble or Instant Coffee	107
1670515	Beer	820
2527500	Writing Paper	210
2560500	Wall Paper	247
3762430	Bras	199
4613500	Perfume, cologne, etc.	212
7002946	Leather footwear for work, over $6.80 per pair	136
7003522	Leather athletic ftwr., male, not spec. prov. for	1,323
7003552	Lea. ftwr., men, cement soles, not spec. prov. for	445
7004505	Leather athletic ftwr., women & misses, over $2.50	562
7004514	Leather casual footwear, women, over $2.50	240
7004544	Leather footwear, women, cement sole, over $2.50	1,746
7005605	Ski boots, uppers 90% rubber or plastic	102
7005610	Men's athletic footwear, uppers 90% rubber/plastic	139
7005620	Women/misses ath. ftwr., uppers 90% rubber/plastic	89

Consumer Non-Durables (continued)

TSUSA #	Brief Product Description	1988 Imports in Mil. $
7006400	Sneakers with rubber sole affixed, not over $3.00	128
7006700	Sneakers with rubber sole, $3.00 to $6.50	106
7058200	Seamless rub./plastic gloves	392
7060500	Leather flat goods, excld. reptile	153
7066225	Handbags of plastics	187
7084520	Sunglasses over $2.50/dozen	273
7084720	Eyeglasses complete with frames	386
7231565	35mm st. film, color, retail	109
7244510	Audio cassettes, blank	195
7244540	Video cassettes, blank	356
7373000	Stuffed animals over a specific value	553
7510510	Hand-held rain umbrellas	83
7600520	Ball-point pens and pencils	126
7722010	Rubber or plastic bags, etc.	171

Consumer Durables

TSUSA #	Brief Product Description	1988 Imports in Mil. $
6610610	Electric fans, excluding permanently installed	145
6613505	Refrigerator and refrig. freezer, under 6.5 cu. ft.	90
6760510	Elec. Port. typewriter, not automatic, no calcula.	92
6762011	Electronic hand-held or pocket calculator	166
6835020	Shavers with self-contained electric motor	136
6842020	Coffee makers	91
6842500	Microwave ovens	577

Consumer Durables (continued)

TSUSA #	Brief Product Description	1988 Imports in Mil. $
6844805	Electric hair dryers	100
6847023	Loudspeaker with a single speaker, not enclosed	224
6847025	Loudspeakers, multi-speaker	179
6847030	Audio-frequency elec. amp.	306
6849252	13 inch color TV's	526
6849258	18 and 19 inch color TV's	327
6851215	AM/FM solid state, broad band radio receivers for motor vehicle installation	147
6851430	Ster. radio without spkrs., excluding batt. operated	241
6853905	Telephone announce and record machines	339
6854052	VCR's	2,506
6869030	Household and other lamps	86
6921014	New 4-cyl. autos other than station wag. & vans	20,974
6921015	Autos over 4 but not over 6 cylinders	9,193
6921030	Autos over 6 cylinders	2,419
7085200	Prism binoculars	91
7150509	Watch, 0 to 1 jewel, case of precious metal	425
7250320	Grand pianos	100
7255000	Music boxes	91
7301900	Pistols and revolvers over $8.00	77
7311520	Fishing rods	86
7312400	Fishing reels, over $8.45	90
7321800	Bicycles over 25 in., under 36 in., over $16.66	236
7322400	Bicycles ov. 25 in., over $16.66, not else. spec.	96
7350215	Snow skis	76

Intermediate Goods

TSUSA #	Brief Product Description	1988 Imports in Mil. $
3558100	Woven or knit Fabric, 70% rubber or plastic	82
4011000	Benzene	115
4017200	Toulene	98
4210800	Sodium Hydroxide	144
4225220	Uranium Fluorides	851
4460540	Rubber milk or latex	126
4461516	Polybutadiene rubber	80
4737000	Titanium dioxide	292
5176100	Electrodes, partially carbon or graphite	81
6103955	Steel pipe, unalloyed, welded, not casing	127
6421110	Steel wire strand, brass plated	172
6465400	Bolts, bolts and nut	193
6465600	Nuts of iron or steel	263
6466320	Cap screw with diameter over 24 inches	157
6604850	Piston-type auto, truck & bus engine, excld. diesel	1,092
6609702	Motor vehicle pumps for liquids	200
6610900	Air con. & refrg. compres., 1/4 hp or less	176
6611020	Air con. & refrg. compres., 1/4 hp to 1 hp	121
6836010	Battery charging generators and alternators	188
6836060	Spark plugs	79
6850200	Tuners for TV receivers	124
6859026	Snap-action switches	80
6859034	Relays with contacts under 10 amps	153
6859036	Relays with contacts over 10 amps	92

Intermediate Goods (continued)

TSUSA #	Brief Product Description	1988 Imports in Mil. $
6880465	Insulated power cable, less than 601 volt capacity	221
6922052	Truck chassis under 19,500 lb., excluding gas	193
6922056	Truck chassis, 26,000 to 33,000 lb.	85
7231507	Medical x-ray film, unexposed	120
7233030	Silver halide paper for color picture negatives	315
7714310	Polyester film, shts., etc.	203
7714312	Pvc film, strips and sheets	235
7725109	New auto tires, radial	1,091
7725136	Other truck and bus tires, radial	600
7912700	Shoe uppers, cut leather	160

Capital Goods

TSUSA #	Brief Product Description	1988 Imports in Mil. $
6604260	Piston-type diesel engine, excluding auto and mfg.	357
6641056	Hydraulic jacks	95
6640720	Wheel-type front-end loaders	449
6640820	Track-type front-end loaders	191
6747025	Chainsaws	85
6763012	Electrostatic copy machine, indirect process	1,175
6763016	Photocopying machines, not spec. provided for	129
6822540	Electric motors, under 1/40 hp, dc	101
6823505	Electric motors, over 1/10 but under 1 hp, ac	158

Capital Goods (continued)

TSUSA #	Brief Product Description	1988 Imports in Mil. $
6823510	Electric motors, over 1/10 but under 1 hp, dc	110
6836040	Starting motors	157
6923402	Wheel-type agri Tractors, under 20 hp	99
6923406	Wheel-type agri Tractors, 40 to 80 hp	390
6923409	Wheel-type agri Tractors, 80 to 100 hp	156
6923430	Track-type agri Trac., new	120
6944148	Airplane, non-mil., multi-engine, 4,400 - 10,000 lb.	164
7082320	Photographic lenses mounted	199

Appendix D

Pass-Through: Second-Degree PDL Model

The reader should note that the product/country combinations whose pass-through rates are reported in Table D.1 were grouped according to the following guidelines: (1) *Group 1* had a significant t-statistic for the 2nd degree polynomial constraint without correcting for excessive serial correlation and had two or more exchange rate coefficients with significant t-ratios, (2) *Group 2* had a significant t-statistic for the 2nd degree PDL constraint after correcting for serial correlation and had two or more exchange rate coefficients with significant t-ratios prior to the correction for serial correlation, and (3) *Group 3* had a significant t-statistic for the 2nd degree PDL constraint after correcting for serial correlation and at least two significant exchange rate coefficients after this correction. However, this group had no significant exchange rate coefficients prior to the correction for serial correlation.

Table D.1

Pass-Through for Products
Fitting the PDL Model

Group One

Product	Country	Pass-Through
Beer	Netherlands	79
Insulated Cable	Mexico	30
40 to 80 HP Tractor	U.K.	69

Group Two

Product	Country	Pass-Through
Bolts and Bolt/Nut	Japan	90
8 cylinder autos	W. Germany	100

Group Three

Product	Country	Pass-Through
Telephone Answering Machine	Japan	18
PVC film, strips, and sheets	Japan	15
Titanium Dioxide	U.K.	33
Leather Footwear for Women	Brazil	29
Air Cond. & Refrig. Compr.	Italy	18
Unalloyed St. Pipe, no cas.	Canada	145
Leather work footwear	Korea	2
Microwave Ovens	Korea	61
Uranium Flourides	Canada	37
Radial Tires, Truck & Bus	Canada	162
Radial Tires, Truck & Bus	France	-36
Truck Chassis, Diesel	France	-27

Appendix E

End-Point Pass-Through:
Product by Country

Japan

Product Description	10/78-4/80	4/80-1/81	1/81-10/82	10/82-9/85	9/85-12/88
Benzene				-5.59	-.30
Toulene					-.25
Polybutadiene rubber	-.25	.68	-.32	-.25	-.10
Electrodes, partially carbon or graphite	-1.66	.39	-1.17	-2.13	-.09
Steel pipe, unalloyed, welded, not casing	-.52	.17	.59	-.46	.70
Steel wire strand, brass plated	-.71	-.15	-.02	-1.06	.52
Bolts, bolts and nut	.32	.38	.31	.78	1.78
Nuts of iron or steel	.62	1.26	.48	1.56	.70
Cap screw with dia. over 24 inches	.19	.59	.42	1.16	.27
Piston-type diesel engine, excluding auto and mfg.				2.93	.31
Piston-type auto., truck and bus engine, exclud. diesel	2.04	.95	.05	.48	.40
Air cond. & refrig. compres., ov. 1/4 hp, not over 1 hp				-.43	.12
Wheel-type front-end loaders					.16

153

Japan (continued)

Product Description	10/78-4/80	4/80-1/81	1/81-10/82	10/82-9/85	9/85-12/88
Chainsaws	-.45				
Portable typewriter, elec., not automatic, no calcula.	-.01	.36	-.46	-2.98	
Electronic hand-held or pocket calculator	1.27	-.17	.06	-2.15	.18
Electrostat. copy mch., indirect process	-.31	-.54	.27	-1.59	.39
Photocopying machines, nspf	.25	-.31	.40	1.28	.49
Electric motors, under 1/40 hp, dc	-3.19	2.18	-2.88	-1.97	.70
Battery charging gen. and alternators				-1.52	.57
Starting motors	.95	-.25	-1.37	-.87	.27
Spark plugs	.03	.43	.09	.33	.34
Microwave ovens	.02	-.12	.24	-3.95	-.14
Loudspeaker with a single speaker, not enclosed			1.88	2.91	.23
Loudspeakers, multiple multi-speaker type			-.86	1.40	-.21
Audio-freq. elec. amp.		1.30	.36	1.76	.85
AM/FM solid st., broad band radio rec. for motor veh. install.	.08	.90	.18	.47	.62
Stereo rad. w/o spkrs., excld. battery oper.	-.04	-.07	1.06	-2.11	1.07
Telephone announce and record machines	.28	.82	.96	-1.71	-.18
VCR's	-.03	.13	1.28	-2.22	-.09
Relays with contacts under 10 amps	-.05	.19	.54	-.16	
Relays with contacts over 10 amps	-1.29	-.16	.77	2.03	-.15

Japan (continued)

Product Description	10/78- 4/80	4/80- 1/81	1/81- 10/82	10/82- 9/85	9/85- 12/88
New 4-cyl. autos other than sta. wag. & vans	.20	.79	-.22	-.54	.24
Autos over 4 but not over 6 cylinders	-.73	.59	-.55	.53	.64
Truck chassis, 26,000 to 33,000 lb.					1.04
Wheel-type agri Tractor under 20 hp		1.40	.30	.47	.48
Wheel-type agri Tractor 40 to 80 hp					1.11
Track-type agri Tractor				-4.65	.10
Photo. lenses mounted	1.56	.73	.57	-.01	1.41
Eyeglasses complete with frames	-1.52	2.23	-.35	3.11	.36
Prism binoculars	-.33	-.10	.73	.40	1.05
Watch, 0 to 1 jewel, case of prec. metal	.63	-.31	1.57	3.32	.82
Med. x-ray film, unexp.	-2.23	1.03	1.81	3.83	-.28
35mm film, col., retail	1.34	-1.13	-.62	.61	.23
Silver halide paper for color picture neg.	-.54	-.38	.65	-.34	-.14
Audio cassettes, blank	.06	.52	-.44	.58	-.24
Video cassettes, blank	.90	.08	1.02	-3.47	.06
Grand pianos	.32	.41	-1.15	-.17	.47
Music boxes	-.19	.50	.31	-.98	.66
Fish. reels, over $8.45				-1.34	-.29	.20
Bicycles ov. 25", under 36", over $16.66	.24	1.47	.39	-.08	1.22
Bicycles over 25", over $16.66, nes				-3.28	.97
Ball-pt. pens & pencils	.06	.20	-1.00	-2.08	.05
Poly. film, sheets, etc	-.64	.33	-1.13	-.07	.16
Pvc film, strp. & sheet	-1.07	.04	-.06	.07	.52
New auto tires, radial	-.04	.50	.06	-.97	.20
Other truck and bus tires			.19	-1.71	.33

Taiwan

Product Description	1/78- 9/79	9/79- 9/83	9/83- 12/88	1/78- 12/88
Woven or knit Fabric,	1.55	-2.09	-.10	1.54
70% rubber or plastic				
Bolts, bolts and nut	2.98	.90	.75	1.57
Nuts of iron or steel	4.75	.57	2.29	5.52
Cap screw with diameter	1.72	1.19	3.46	4.20
over 24 inches				
Electric fans, excluding		1.37		
permanently installed				
Hydraulic jacks		-.08	1.11	
Electronic hand-held or	-.54	3.18	.56	-1.33
pocket calculator				
Electric motors, under	1.63	-5.53	.77	6.25
1/40 hp, dc				
Electric hair dryers		-1.70	-.41	
Loudspeaker with a single		-7.81	-.10	
speaker, not enclosed				
Loudspeakers, multiple	.46	-7.98	-.41	2.86
multi-speaker type				
Audio-frequency elec. amp.			.46	
13 inch color TV's	.88	.76	.23	.38
18 and 19 in. color TV'	.22	.18	-.25	-.33
Tuners for TV receivers	2.11	-7.34	.72	8.05
VCR's			.89	
Household and other lamps			.32	
Insul. power cable, less	5.77	.83	.36	2.01
than 601 volt capacity				
Leather footwear for work,		-.52	.78	
over $6.80 per pair				
Leather ath. footwear,	4.41	-.73	1.65	5.93
male, nspf				
Leather ftwr. for men,	3.67	-1.43	1.28	5.41
cement soles, nspf				
Leather ath. ftwr., wmn.	-1.00	-.11	2.47	2.53
& misses, over $2.50				

Taiwan (continued)

Product Description	1/78-9/79	9/79-9/83	9/83-12/88	1/78-12/88
Leather casual footwear, women, over $2.50	7.44	2.07	.82	1.93
Leather ftwr., women, cement sole, over $2.50	6.06	.93	.63	2.52
Men's ath. ftwr., uppers 90% rubber/plastic	3.11	.03	1.58	3.94
Women/misses ath. ftwr., uppers 90% rub./plastic	9.06	.46	.81	4.78
Sneakers with rubber sole affixed, not over $3.00		-3.09	-.55	
Sneakers with rubber sole, $3.00 to $6.50		1.34	-.01	
Seamless rub./plas. gloves			2.22	
Handbags of plastics	4.53	.91	.86	2.36
Sunglasses > $2.50/dz.	.47	.02	-.15	-.06
Prism binoculars			2.17	.95
Music boxes	3.47	-.60	.72	3.14
Fishing rods	-1.70	-.02	1.24	2.31
Bicycles over 25 in., un. 36 in., over $16.66	-.42	-1.39	.91	3.64
Bicycles over 25 in., over $16.66, nes		-7.41	2.47	6.35
Stuffed animals over a specific value	-1.03	-6.02	5.10	
Hand-held rain umbrellas	1.76	-.04	1.82	3.56
Pvc film, strips and shts.	2.69	-.66	.36	2.07
Rubber or plas. bags, etc.	3.16	-2.87	.54	4.56

Korea

Product Description	1/80- 9/85	9/85- 12/88	1/80- 12/88
Wall Paper	1.05	.30	.67
Refrig. and refrig. frzr. under 6.5 cu. ft.	-.07	.84	-1.18
Battery charging gen. and alternators		.19	
Microwave ovens	1.79	-.38	
Loudspeaker with a single speaker, not enclosed	-9.69	-1.69	-8.70
Audio-frequency elec. amp.	-2.40	.06	
13 inch color TV's	.74	-.07	.82
18 and 19 inch color TV's	.71	-.21	.79
Telephone announce and record machines	.80	-.33	15.46
VCR's	2.50	-.52	
Household and other lamps	-3.23	.70	
New 4-cylinder autos other than station wag. & vans		.91	
Leather footwear for work, over $6.80 per pair	-.73	.64	-3.16
Leather athletic footwear, male, nspf	-.70	1.39	-4.91
Leather footwear for men, cement soles, nspf	.18	.88	-1.65
Leather ath. ftwr., women & misses, over $2.50	-1.29	.87	-3.82
Women/misses ath. ftwr., uppers 90% rub./plas.		2.72	
Sneakers with rubber sole affixed, not over $3.00	-.01	.38	
Sneakers with rubber sole, $3.00 to $6.50	-.27	-.11	
Leather flat goods, excluding reptile	1.36	.39	-.19
Handbags of plastics	-.08	.46	-2.55
Photogr. lenses mounted	-.80	.67	-3.51

Korea (continued)

Product Description	1/80-9/85	9/85-12/88	1/80-12/88
Sunglasses over $2.50/dz.	.65	1.84	-.45
Prism binoculars	.91	.37	.23
Audio cassettes, blank	-.45	-.98	
Video cassettes, blank		-.85	
Grand pianos	-.73	.26	-2.19
Fishing rods	.10	.88	-2.32
Fishing reels, over $8.45	.63	.86	
Bicycles over 25 in., un. 36 in., over $16.66	-.07	.01	-1.01
Bicycles over 25 in., over $16.66, nes		-.63	
Stuffed animals over a specific value	.15		
Poly. film, sheets, etc.	.19	1.67	

Canada

Product Description	1/78- 1/86	1/86- 12/88	1/78- 12/88
Beer	-2.82	.62	-9.95
Writing Paper	-.21	1.81	-4.79
Wall Paper	-1.92	1.22	-9.08
Woven or knit Fabric, 70% rubber or plastic	-2.67	.25	-8.20
Benzene	1.16	-.30	9.03
Toulene	-5.59	.12	-15.89
Sodium Hydroxide	1.19	.39	2.60
Uranium Fluorides	2.87	-1.62	54.59
Polybutadiene rubber	-2.02	-.17	-5.01
Titanium dioxide	-2.10	.82	-8.42
Steel pipe, unalloyed, welded, not casing	-.38	2.45	-6.92
Bolts, bolts and nut	-1.63	.52	-6.01
Cap screw with diameter over 24 inches	-.80	.50	-3.48
Wheel-type frt.-end ldrs.	.81	.47	
Electric motors, over 1/10 but under 1 hp, dc	-2.16	.07	-3.66
Insul. power cable, less than 601 volt capacity	.77	3.40	-4.20
Pvc film, strips and shts.	.50	.33	.73
Rub. or plastic bags, etc.	-.21	1.02	-2.92
New auto tires, radial	.54	.29	.90
Other truck and bus tires, radial	-.27	2.54	

W. Germany

Product Description	1/78- 1/80	1/80- 3/85	3/85- 12/88	1/78- 12/88
Beer	.71	-.26	.03	1.67
Wall Paper	-.22	.68	.97	.93
Titanium dioxide	.41	-.21	.60	4.07
Steel wire strand, brass plated			.83	
Piston-type auto., truck & bus eng., excld. diesel	1.24	-.14	1.12	8.34
Motor vehicle pumps for liquids		-.44		
Chainsaws	1.58	.60	.85	3.37
Battery charging gen. and alternators		-.27	.37	
Starting motors	1.50	.43	.28	1.63
Spark plugs	.78	.12	.56	3.18
Coffee makers		.54	.40	
Relays with contacts over 10 amps			1.57	
Autos over 4 but not over 6 cylinders	2.84	.10	.91	10.05
Autos over 6 cylinders	3.21	.20	1.11	
Wheel-type agri Tractors, 40 to 80 hp		.51	.28	
Wheel-type agri Tractors, 80 to 100 hp		-.26		
Silver halide paper for color picture negatives	-.44	.30	.01	-1.12
Pvc film, strips and shts.	1.61	.22	.48	3.58
New auto tires, radial	1.35	.55	.32	1.17

Mexico

Product Description	1/78- 12/88
Cocoa Butter	.27
Beer	-.41
Writing Paper	-.77
Bras	-.87
Polybutadiene rubber	-.19
Piston-type auto., truck & bus eng., exclud. diesel	-.32
Refrig. and refrig. frzr., under 6.5 cu. ft.	-.13
Electric motors, over 1/10 but under 1 hp, ac	-1.13
Electric motors, over 1/10 but under 1 hp, dc	-.82
Battery charging gen. and alternators	-.08
13 inch color TV's	-.01
18 and 19 inch color TV's	-.54
AM/FM solid state, broad band radio receivers for motor vehicle installation	-.15
Snap-action switches	.14
Relays with contacts under 10 amps	-.32
Insul. power cable, less than 601 volt capacity	.01
Audio cassettes, blank	-.12
Shoe uppers, cut leather	.06

Brazil

Product Description	1/78-12/88
Cocoa Butter	.43
Soluble or Instant Coffee	.71
Writing Paper	1.00
Air cond. & refrig. compres., 1/4 hp or less	.05
AM/FM solid st., brd. band radio rec. for motor vehicle installation	-.12
Truck chassis, 26,000 to 33,000 lb.	.20
Leather footwear for men, cement soles, nspf	-.37
Leather casual footwear, women, over $2.50	-.17
Leather footwear, women, cement sole, over $2.50	-.48
Silver halide paper for color picture negatives	.01
Pistols and revolvers over $8.00	-.78
Shoe uppers, cut leather	-.09

Hong Kong

Product Description	1/78- 9/83	9/83- 12/88	5/86- 4/87	1/78- 12/88
Electronic hand-held or pocket calculator	1.11	1.91	6.98	-1.20
Electric motors, under 1/40 hp, dc	-3.00	1.39	2.20	-21.54
Coffee makers		47.88		
Electric hair dryers	.23	-1.33	.27	
Telephone announce and record machines		-2.24	.03	
Leather casual footwear, women, over $2.50	-2.36	.35	1.86	-11.82
Watch, 0 to 1 jewel, case of precious metal	1.78	3.48	.34	-1.04
Audio cassettes, blank	-.05	1.25	-2.12	-5.25
Video cassettes, blank		4.57		
Music boxes	-1.90	1.01	8.92	-13.53
Hand-held rain umbrellas	-.78	.95	2.56	-7.64

Singapore

Product Description	1/78- 12/81	12/81- 2/85	2/85- 12/88	1/78- 12/88
Cocoa Butter	1.95	2.78	.80	.36
Steel pipe, unalloyed, welded, not casing		7.28		
Air cond. & refrig. compres., 1/4 hp or less	3.74	1.66	-.39	1.04
Port. typewriter, elec., not auto., no calculator	3.78	.65	-4.05	.59
Microwave ovens	1.13	2.26	-1.57	
13 inch color TV's	-2.20	2.14	.05	-2.43
Telephone announce and record machines		.79	.24	

United Kingdom

Product Description	1/78-1/81	1/81-3/85	3/85-12/88	1/78-12/88
Wall Paper	1.91	.49	.17	-3.65
Titanium dioxide	1.83	-.03	.84	-22.68
Motor vehicle pumps for liquids			1.13	
Autos over 4 but not over 6 cylinders	3.34	-.36	.22	-5.99
Wheel-type agri tractors under 20 hp		.54	1.32	
Wheel-type agri tractors 40 to 80 hp	2.27	.16		
Wheel-type agri Tractors, 80 to 100 hp			3.09	
Airplane, non-mil., multi-eng., 4,400 - 10,000 lb.			.69	
35mm film, color, retail		.70	.05	
Poly. film, sheets, etc.	.32	-.98	-.39	-4.52

Italy

Product Description	1/78-1/80	1/80-3/85	3/85-12/88	1/78-12/88
Wall Paper		-.12	-.10	
Steel wire strand, brass plated	1.51	.02	-.03	-.28
Air cond. & refrig. compr., 1/4 hp or less	2.52	.25	.36	-.75
Leather ftwr. for men, cement soles, nspf	10.00	.51	1.08	-3.31
Ski boots, uppers 90% rubber or plastic	-.73	-.30	.32	-1.01
Leather flat goods, excluding reptile	-7.57	.10	1.55	.98
Eyeglasses complete with frames	5.88	-.13	1.38	-5.97
New auto tires, radial	1.28	.24	.23	.57

France

Product Description	1/78- 1/80	1/80- 3/85	3/85- 12/88	1/78- 12/88
Perfume, cologne, etc.	5.13	.49	-.27	-.35
Titanium dioxide	1.16	-.32	.87	-5.96
Track-type front-end ldrs.		.24		
Truck chassis under 19,500 lb., excluding gas		-.11	.16	
Snow skis	4.51	.46	.09	-2.11
New auto tires, radial	1.63	.64	.23	.45
Other truck and bus tires, radial		.60	.18	

Spain

Product Description	1/78- 1/80	1/80- 3/85	3/85- 12/88	1/78- 12/88
Steel wire strand, brass plated		.10	.21	
Leather ftwr. for men, cement soles, nspf	2.30	.10	.86	-4.95
Leather ftwr., women, cement sole, over $2.50	3.02	.14	.57	-3.62
Snow skis		-.13	.62	
New auto tires, radial	-.18	.46	.46	.45

Malaysia

Product Description	1/78- 9/80	9/80- 12/88	7/86- 5/87	1/78- 12/88
Cocoa Butter	.96	2.22	-.23	3.39
Rubber milk or latex	6.56	-1.53	4.44	-10.89
13 inch color TV's		1.91	-.19	
Tuners for TV receivers		-2.83		

Netherlands

Product Description	1/78-1/80	1/80-3/85	3/85-12/88	1/78-12/88
Beer	1.45	.58	.79	3.77
Photocopying mch., nspf		.59	.56	
Shavers with self-contained electric motor	.66	.07	.42	3.42

Sweden

Product Description	1/78-1/80	1/80-3/85	3/85-12/88	1/78-12/88
Chainsaws	.93	-.01	.82	-2.68
New 4-cyl. autos other than station wag. & vans	2.34	-1.26	.78	-9.31
Fishing reels, over $8.45			.72	.93

Philippines

Product Description	1/78-12/88
Bras	-1.27

References

Aaker, David A. and George S. Day, *Marketing Research*, 3rd edition, Wiley, New York, 1986.

Baldwin, Richard, "Hysteresis in Import Prices: The Beachhead Effect," *American Economic Review*, Sept. 1988, pp. 773-85.

Baldwin, Richard and Paul Krugman, "Persistent Trade Effects of Large Exchange Rate Shocks," *Quarterly Journal of Economics*, November 1989, pp. 635-654.

Belsley, David A., Edwin Kuh, and Ray E. Welsch, *Regression Diagnostics*, New York, Wiley, 1980.

Branson, William H., "The Trade Effects of the 1971 Currency Realignments," *Brookings Papers on Economic Activity*, 1: 1972, pp. 15-58, and in the same volume, L.R. Klein, "Comments and Discussion," pp. 59-65.

Cassidy, Henry J., *Using Econometrics: A Beginner's Guide*, Reston Publishing Co., Inc., Reston, Va., 1981.

Clark, Peter B., "The Effects of Recent Exchange Rate Changes on the U.S. Trade Balance," in P.B. Clark, D.E. Logue, and R.J. Sweeney, eds., *The Effects of Exchange Rate Adjustments*, U.S. Treasury, OASIA Research Department, 1974.

Devine, P.J., et al, *An Introduction to Industrial Economics*, 4th edition, 1985.

Devinney, Timothy, *Issues in Pricing: Theory and Research*, Lexington Books, Lexington, MA, 1988.

Deyak, Timothy A., Charles W. Sawyer, and Richard L. Sprinkle, "An Empirical Examination of the Structural Stability of Disaggregated U.S. Import Demand," *Review of Economic Studies*, 1989, pp. 337-341.

Dohner, Robert S., "Export Pricing, Flexible Exchange Rates, and Divergence in the Prices of Traded Goods," *Journal of International Economics*, February 1984, pp. 79-101.

Dornbusch, Rudiger, "Exchange Rates and Prices," *American Economic Review*, March 1987, pp. 93-106.

Dunn, Robert M., "Flexible Exchange Rates and Oligopoly Pricing: A Study of Canadian Markets," *Journal of Political Economy*, Vol. 78 (1970), pp. 140-51.

Feenstra, Robert C., "Symmetric Pass-Through of Tariffs and Exchange Rates Under Imperfect Competition: An Empirical Test," *Journal of International Economics*, Vol. 27 (1989), pp. 25-45.

Feinberg, Robert C., "The Effects of Foreign Exchange Movements on U.S. Domestic Prices," *Review of Economics and Statistics*, 1989, pp. 505-511.

Feinberg, Robert C., "The Interaction of Market Power and Exchange Rate Effects on German Domestic Prices," *Journal of International Economics*, September 1986, pp. 61-70.

Fieleke, Norman S., "Dollar Appreciation and U.S. Import Prices," *New England Economic Review*, November/December 1985, pp. 49-54.

Fisher, Eric, "A Model of Exchange Rate Pass-Through," *Journal of International Economics*, Vol. 26 (1989), pp. 119-137.

Froot, Kenneth A., and Paul D. Klemperer, "Exchange Rate Pass-Through When Market Share Matters," *American Economic Review*, September 1989, pp. 637-654.

Gagnon, Joseph E., and Michael M. Knetter, "Pricing to Market in International Trade: Evidence from Panel Data on Automobiles and Total Merchandise," *NBER Summer Workshop on International Monetary Affairs*, 1990.

Giovannini, Alberto, "Exchange Rates and Traded Goods Prices," *Journal of International Economics*, Vol. 24 (1988), pp. 45-68.

Goldstein, M. and M.S. Khan, "Income and Price Effects in Foreign Trade," in Ronald W. Jones and Peter B. Kenen, eds., *Handbook of International Economics*, vol. II, North-Holland, New York, 1985.

Granger, Clive W. and P. Newbold, "Spurious Regressions in Econometrics," *Journal of Econometrics*, 2: 1974, pp. 111-120.

Haberler, G., "The Market for Foreign Exchange and the Stability of the Balance of Payments: A Theoretical Analysis," *Kyklos*, Vol. 3 (1949), pp. 193-218.

Hafer, Richard W., "Does Dollar Depreciation Cause Inflation?" *Federal Reserve Bank of St. Louis Review*, July/August 1989.

Hamada, Koichi and Akiyoshi Horiuchi, "Monetary, Financial and Real Effects of Yen Internationalization," in J. David Richardson and Sven Arndt, eds., *Real Financial Linkages Among Open Economies*, MIT Press, Cambridge, 1987.

Hatter, Victoria, The Behavior of U.S. Export Prices and Profit Margins, 1981-1986, Staff Report, Office of Trade and Investment Analysis, International Trade Administration, U.S. Dept. of Commerce, October 1987, Project DIE-005-87.

Helkie, W. L. and Peter Hooper, "An Empirical Analysis of the External Deficit, 1980-86," in Ralph C. Bryant, Gerald Holtham, and Peter Hooper, eds., *External Deficits and the Dollar*, the Brookings Institution, Washington, D.C., 1988.

Hendry, David F. and Grayham E. Mizon, "Serial Correlation as a Convenient Simplification, Not a Nuisance: A Comment on a Study of the Demand for Money by the Bank of England," *The Economic Journal*, September 1978, pp. 549-563.

Herd, Richard, Import and Export Price Equations for Manufactures, Working paper #43, OECD, Department of Economics and Statistics, Balance of Payments Division, June 1987.

Hicks, J.R., *Value and Capital*, Clarendon Press, Oxford, 1939.

Hooper, Peter and Steven W. Kohlhagen, "The Effect of Exchange Rate Uncertainty on the Prices and the Volume of International Trade," *Journal of International Economics*, November 1978, pp. 483-511.

Hooper, Peter and Barbara R. Lowrey, "Impact of the Dollar Depreciation on the U.S. Price Level: An Analytical Survey of Empirical Estimates," Staff Study 103, Washington, Board of Governors of the Federal Reserve System, March, 1978.

Hooper, Peter and Catherine Mann, "Exchange Rate Pass-Through in the 1980's: The Case of U.S. Imports of Manufactures," *Brookings Papers on Economic Activity*, 1:1989, pp. 297-337.

Hooper, Peter and Catherine Mann, The Emergence and Persistence of the U.S. External Imbalance, 1980-87, *Princeton Studies in International Finance*, No. 65, October 1989.

International Currency Analysis, Inc., *World Currency Yearbook*, various issues.

International Monetary Fund, *International Financial Statistics*, various issues.

Isard, Peter, "The Price Effects of Exchange-Rate Changes," in P.B. Clark, D.E. Logue and R.J. Sweeney, eds., *The Effects of Exchange Rate Adjustments*, U.S. Treasury, OASIA Research Department, 1974.

Isard, Peter, "How Far Can We Push the 'Law of One Price'?" *American Economic Review*, December 1977, pp. 942-948.

Kenen, Peter B. and C. Pack, "Exchange Rates and Domestic Prices: A Survey of the Evidence," Research Memorandum, International Finance Section, Princeton University, Princeton, 1980.

Kennedy, Peter, *A Guide to Econometrics*, second edition, MIT Press, Cambridge, MA, 1985.

Kim, Yoonbai, "Exchange Rates and Import Prices in the United States: A Varying-Parameter Estimation of Exchange Rate Pass-Through," *Journal of Business and Economic Statistics*, July 1990, pp. 305-315.

Kmenta, Jan, *Elements of Econometrics*, 2nd edition, Macmillan, New York, 1986.

Knetter, Michael M., "Price Discrimination by U.S. and German Exporters," *American Economic Review*, March 1989, pp. 198-210.

Kravis, Irving B. and Robert Lipsey, "Price Behavior in the Light of Balance of Payments Theories," *Journal of International Economics*, May 1978, pp. 193-246.

Kravis, Irving B. and Robert Lipsey, "Export Prices and Transmission of Inflation," *American Economic Review*, February 1977, pp. 155-163.

Kreinin, Mordechai E., "The Effect of Exchange Rate Changes on the Prices and Volume of Foreign Trade," *IMF Staff Papers*, July 1977, 2: pp. 297-329.

Kreinin, Mordechai, Stephen Martin and E.J. Sheehey, "Differential Response of U.S. Import Prices and Quantities to Exchange-Rate Adjustments," *Weltwirtschaftliches Archiv.*, 1987 (123) 3 pp. 449-462.

Krugman, Paul, *Exchange-Rate Instability*, MIT Press, Cambridge, Mass., 1989.

Krugman, Paul, "The Delinking of Exchange Rates from Reality," and "Pricing to Market When the Exchange Rate Changes," in Sven W. Arndt and J. David Richardson, eds., *Real Financial Linkages Among Open Economies*, MIT Press, Cambridge, Mass., 1987.

Krugman, Paul and Richard Baldwin, "The Persistence of the U.S. Trade Deficit," *Brookings Papers on Economic Activity*, 1987 (1), pp. 1-55.

Llewellyn, G.E.J., "The Determinants of United Kingdom Import Prices," *Economic Journal*, 1974, pp. 18-31.

Magee, Stephen P., "U.S. Import Prices in the Currency Contract Period," *Brookings Papers on Economic Activity*, 1: 1974, pp. 117-164.

Magee, Stephen P., "Currency Contracts, Pass Through, and Devaluation," *Brookings Papers on Economic Activity*, 1: 1973, pp. 303-325.

Mann, Catherine L., "The Effects of Exchange Rate Trends and Volatility on Export Prices: Industry Examples from Japan, Germany and the United States," *Weltwirtschaftliches Archiv*, 1989, pp. 588-617.

Mann, Catherine L., "Prices, Profit Margins, and Exchange Rates," *Federal Reserve Bulletin*, June 1986, pp. 366-379.

Marston, Richard C., "Pricing to Market in Japanese Manufacturing," National Bureau of Economic Research, Working Paper No. 2905, March 1989.

Marston, Richard C., "Price Behavior in Japanese and U.S. Manufacturing," National Bureau of Economic Research, Working Paper No. 3364, May 1990.

Mastropasqua, Cristina and Stefano Vona, "The U.S. Current Account Imbalance and the Dollar: The Issue of the Exchange Rate Pass-Through," Banka D'Italia No. 120, June 1989.

McKinnon, Ronald, *Money in International Exchange*, New York, Oxford University Press, 1979.

Melick, Will, "Single Equation Estimates of Exchange Rate Pass-Through," Eastern Economic Association Annual Meetings, March 1990.

Moffett, Michael H., "The J-curve Revisited: An Empirical Examination for the U.S.," *Journal of International Money and Finance*, Vol. 8 (1989), pp. 425-444.

Monroe, Kent B. and Tridib Mazumdar, "Pricing-Decision Models: Recent Developments and Research Opportunities," in Timothy M. Devinney, editor, *Issues in Pricing: Theory and Research*, Lexington Books, Lexington, MA, 1988.

Norton, Robert E., "The Dollar: How Low Should it Go?", *Fortune*, December 7, 1987, pp. 38-44.

Officer, Lawrence H., "The Relationship Between the Absolute and the Relative PPP Theory of Cassel," *History of Political Economy*, Vol. 14, no. 2, 1982, pp. 251-255.

Ohno, Kenichi, "Export Pricing Behavior of Manufacturing: A U.S.-Japan Comparison," *IMF Staff Papers*, Vol. 36, No. 3, September 1989.

Pick Publishing Corporation, *Pick's Currency Yearbook*, various issues.

Pierce, David A., "Relationships - and the Lack Thereof - Between Economic Time Series, with Special Reference to Money and Interest Rates," *Journal of the American Statistical Association*, March 1977, pp. 11-22 and a Rejoinder on pp. 24-26.

Richardson, J. David, "Some Empirical Evidence on Commodity Arbitrage and the Law of One Price," *Journal of International Economics*, 1978, pp. 341-351.

Ricks, David A. and Michael Czinkota, "International Business: An Examination of the Corporate Viewpoint," *Journal of International Business Studies*, Fall 1979, pp. 97-100.

SAS Institute, Inc., *SAS User's Guide: Basics*, Version 5 Edition, SAS Institute, Inc., Cary, NC, 1985.

SAS Institute, Inc., *SAS User's Guide: Statistics*, Version 5 Edition, SAS Institute, Inc., Cary, NC, 1985.

SAS Institute, INC., *SAS/ETS User's Guide*, Version 6, first edition, SAS Institute, Inc., Cary, NC, 1988.

Scherer, Frederic M., *Industrial Market Structure and Economic Performance*, 2nd edition, Rand-McNally College Publishing, Chicago, 1980.

Schwartz, L. and L. Perez, "Survey Evidence on the Pass-Through of Smithsonian Revaluations," in P.B. Clark, D.E. Logue, and R.J. Sweeney, eds., *The Effects of Exchange Rate Adjustments*, U.S. Treasury, OASIA Research Department, 1974.

Spitaller, Erich, "Short Run Effects of Exchange Rate Changes on Terms of Trade and Trade Balance," *IMF Staff Papers*, 1980, pp. 320-348.

United Nations, *Yearbook of Industrial Statistics*, 1974-1981 issues.

United Nations, *Industrial Statistics Yearbook*, 1982- 1988 issues.

U.S. Department of Commerce, *Import Prices*, various issues from 1978-1988.

U.S. Department of Labor, Bureau of Labor Statistics, *Producer Price Indexes*, various issues.

U.S. Department of the Treasury, Customs Service, *Importing into the United States*, January 1989, Customs Publication No. 504.

Williams, D., "Estimating in Levels or First Differences: A Defence of the Method Used for Certain Demand-For-Money Equations," *The Economic Journal*, September 1978, pp. 564-568.

Wilson, John F. and Wendy E. Takacs, "Differential Responses to Price and Exchange Rate Influences in the Foreign Trade of Selected Industrial Countries," *Review of Economics and Statistics*, May 1979, pp. 267-279.

Woo, Wing T., "Exchange Rates and the Prices of Nonfood, Nonfuel Products," *Brookings Papers on Economic Activity*, 2: 1984, pp. 511-536.

Index